The Wholefood Harvest Cookbook

Gourmet recipes from garden to table

Written by Rachel Hunt

Illustrated by Paula Cloonan

**Foreword by Tom Jaine, editor,
The Good Food Guide**

GALLERY BOOKS
An Imprint of W. H. Smith Publishers Inc.
112 Madison Avenue
New York City 10016

First published in the United States in 1990 by Gallery Books,
an imprint of W. H. Smith Publishers, Inc.,
112 Madison Avenue, New York, New York 10016.

Gallery Books are available for bulk purchase for sales
promotions and premium use. For details write or telephone
the Manager of Special Sales. W. H. Smith Publishers, Inc.,
112 Madison Avenue, New York, New York 10016. (212) 532-6600.

0–8317–9444–5

Typeset by Northern Phototypesetting Company Limited, Bolton, England.
Printed in Spain by Graficas Estella sa.

CONTENTS

Ashley & Rachelle at Country Fayre

FOREWORD

If our grandparents had been told in their youth that by the 1990s a large part of the population would have given up eating meat and fish and found happiness instead with vegetables and fruit, they would have snickered in disbelief – unless they knew that those people had beards, wore sandals and grew their own tobacco. Then, wholefood and vegetarianism was the concern of a few; now, it may become the preference of a near-majority.

Yet our grandparents had their advantages then which we, helped by books like Rachel Hunt's, try ever so hard to re-create in our capsuled, big-city life. They had the seasons, they had gardens, they had time; more important, they did not have freezers, microwaves, or supermarkets. The lesson of this book, apparent from its very first page, is that we ignore the rhythms of the earth and we accept the temptation of the twelve-month strawberry at our peril.

When I helped keep a restaurant in a small town by the sea in Devon, Rachel Hunt kept a health-food store nearby. We soon found our feet pounding the path to her door. What her shelves offered was taste; taste in bucketfuls, basket loads of flavour. This marked her produce off from the wan product of the multiples. If you asked for flour, you got it: brown, wheaty and textured, rather than white wallpaper glue. If you used her sugar, you knew it – it tasted of sugar, not some insidious sweetening agent. Some palates pretend sophistication and despise the rough and the brown; what they are often doing is admitting they cannot cope with flavour.

As with wholefoods, so with vegetables and fruit. Flavour is being recognised as important once again. We have got locked into a marketplace conditioned by space, not time. The achievement of bringing beans from Kenya or blackberries from New Zealand ranks higher than cooking and eating by the calendar. Yet these time-bandits usually lack the one thing that should distinguish our food: taste. The appeal of the first of any crop is granted – I think of the noblemen of the 18th century who would pay four times over the odds for early cucumbers, or those courtiers of Louis XIV's Versailles who waited with bated breath for the first peas of the summer – but that is not the same as ignoring the seasons altogether. The delicacy of flavour of the earlies is quite different from the flabbiness of much hothouse rubbish. This book should bring us back to the calendar with a vengeance.

When great chefs are lauded and restaurants praised to the skies, it is often for the complexity and subtlety of their cooking. Recipes are secrets, ingredients legion, yet to what purpose? Alchemists there are who can achieve some new harmony but much of the time the feast is for the eye and the flavour is fugitive. After many a meal, you begin to hanker for the direct approach, the bold tastes, rich textures and splashes of colour that are often better achieved in the home than in the self-conscious restaurant. Rachel gives you the chance to practise this art – a table laden with fresh wholemeal bread, a pale green artichoke and hazelnut soup, lustrous vegetable kebabs and a gleaming raspberry and redcurrant fool will soon set your tastebuds aflame. And if words don't do it, take inspiration from Paula Cloonan's drawings. I did.

Tom Jaine
Editor
GOOD FOOD GUIDE

INTRODUCTION

My initial introduction to vegetarian cooking came twelve years ago when I began working for Cranks, a highly respected vegetarian business. They were pioneers in the setting up of the first vegetarian restaurants in England. After two years with them, I started my own business, and during the following ten years I have run a Health Food shop, a vegetarian restaurant, and given classes in Vegetarian Cooking at the local Community College.

Customers and students have often asked me to write a cook book, and the answer was, 'Maybe one day!' It was not until Paula suggested we produce a book together, basing it on a rural calendar using her illustrations, that I started in earnest to compile this book.

The recipes are often ones which have been frequently requested at my shop. Others have been used in my cooking classes and at my restaurant. I have tried to cover all areas of vegetarian cooking, and I hope anybody who is concerned with their health and environment will find it useful.

There are many recipes suitable for strict vegetarians. As we do not include meat in the recipes they are low fat. Cream has been used in some of the dessert recipes, but this is optional. There is no need to go overboard with its use, but a little will not harm you – unless you feel guilty about eating it! If you get too cranky about food you can make yourself anti-social, especially if people have to think about inviting you for a meal because they are frightened to cook for you.

All the quantities are for six people or for four if they have large appetites.

Rachel Hunt

THE STORE CUPBOARD

As we will be using mostly fresh foods, the store cupboard will contain items to flavour and bulk out meals. Wholefoods do not contain preservatives so careful storage is necessary. Large glass jars are ideal as it's easy to see just exactly what you have in store. The items listed will provide the basis of a variety of meals; you should always be able to muster something in an emergency.

Canned Goods
Tomatoes, tomato purée in cans and tubes.

Beans. You can now get a variety of cooked/canned beans in water – chick peas, haricot beans, butter beans and others. Soya beans are available in tomato sauce but I haven't seen them in water yet. These and chick peas are particularly useful canned as they take such a long time to cook.

Flavourings and Sauces
Shoyu Japanese soya sauce. This is highly concentrated and a good source of protein.

Tamari
This is a sauce fermented in the same way as shoyu but uses rice instead of wheat, so it is suitable as a source of protein to people on gluten-free diets.

Miso
This again is fermented in the same way as shoyu, but in a much more highly concentrated form. It should be added sparingly only after the cooking has been completed. There are three types – MUGI, HACHO and KOME. Mugi is soya; barley hacho is soya alone, so has more protein value; Kome is soya and rice.

Vegetable Stock
This is a matter of personal preference. There are many different ones on the market, in jars or packets. Experimentation is how you will find the ones to work best for you.

Brewers Yeast Cubes
These are handy to have as they add a lot of nourishment to gravies and casseroles.

Spices and Herbs
These are another personal item. The choice is yours, but black peppercorns and sea salt are essential.

Tahini
A paste made from crushed sesame seeds, with a similar taste to peanut butter.

Peanut Butter (page 62)
Use the type without additives.

Vinegars
Mainly used for salad dressings. Cider and wine should suffice.

Oils
Cold pressed are preferable as they contain nutrients lost in the processing of other oils. Here the choice is wide, but sunflower, peanut, olive, safflower or grapeseed should be sufficient choice.

Pasta
Wholewheat, in any shape you fancy.

Rice
Brown short and long grain, perhaps Basmati.

Grains
Buckwheat, millet, rye, wheat, bulgar wheat, couscous, barley, oat flakes.

Flour
Wholewheat plain and self-raising, strong white, granary, rye, barley, soya, rice, potato and corn.

Nuts and Seeds
Almonds, Brazil nuts, cashews, coconut creamed and desiccated, hazels, peanuts, pecans, pine kernels, walnuts, sunflower seeds, sesame seeds, alfalfa seeds, pumpkin seeds.

Beans and Peas
Aduki, butter, black-eyed, chick, pinto, flageolet, lentils, red kidney and haricot.

Dried Fruit
For cake making, packed lunches, muesli and desserts. Apricots, bananas, figs, dates, apple rings, pears, peaches, prunes, currants, sultanas and raisins. Buy the sun-dried varieties.

Sugar
No sugar is good for you, but raw cane sugars do have more minerals than the refined types. Demerara, Muscovado. Alternative sweeteners are molasses, honey, malt extract and maple syrup.

Carob Powder
Used as an alternative to chocolate. Useful for migraine sufferers.

Natural Essences
Almond, Vanilla, Peppermint, Orange.

BASIC KITCHEN EQUIPMENT

You can get away with very little kitchen equipment. Years ago really excellent cooks managed to produce wonderful meals without the array of gadgetry we have available today. Many items in the kitchen have several uses.

In a vegetarian household, where there is a lot of chopping and slicing going on, it could be a wise move to invest in a good food processor. Ask your friends for recommendations to particular types. This piece of equipment has many uses – slicing, chopping, grinding, blending and liquidizing.

Good quality knives
Buy the best you can and they will last for years. Everyone has their favourites – a large chopping knife, a bread knife and a serrated vegetable knife form the nucleus of my collection.

Measuring jug or pitcher

Kitchen scissors
These are useful for all sorts of cutting jobs.

Box grater
Although if you have a processor, you probably will not need one.

Pepper and salt mills

Juice extractor
If you can't afford a really good electric one, an old fashioned lemon-squeezer is probably your best bet.

Garlic press
Some have an olive stoner attached.

Perforated spoons
These are useful for lifting foods out of liquids.

Balloon or bamboo whisk
Absolutely essential. You will never have a lumpy sauce with one of these.

Soup ladle
We will be making much of use of this!

Wooden spoons
Remember not to leave them in the pan with the food cooking, as the flavours permeate the wood.

Spaghetti fork
This is useful but not essential – you may prefer to drain pasta in a colander.

Metal tongs
Thes are useful for lifting and turning food.

Fish slice
This can be used in the same way as tongs; good for turning rissoles in the pan.

Rolling pin

Pastry Brush
I use a paint brush for pastries; they are much more durable. Buy new and wash thoroughly before using.

Wire racks
These are necessary for cooling food.

Mixing bowls and pudding basins
Buy them in a material to suit your taste.

Baking trays, bread tins, cake tins, flan dishes
You will need various shapes and sizes.

Saucepans
Stainless steel are best. Here again get the best you can afford and they will last a lifetime.

Frying pan
Stainless steel again.

Wok
Tremendously useful and very inexpensive to buy. Select one that has a wooden handle for ease of use. It can be used to cook vegetables in a small amount of liquid very quickly.

Can opener, bottle opener and corkscrew

Potato peeler
This can be used for peeling all kinds of root vegetables, and for coring apples.

Skewers
These are useful for kebabs and also for testing to see if cakes are cooked for the less experienced cook.

Casserole dishes
These can double up as gratin dishes.

Fondue Set
I love and use mine quite regularly for entertaining. Great fun for your friends. It is also surprising how filling a fondue can be.

Electric hand mixer
This takes the ache out of cake making.

Sieve or sifter
Sifting flour will make your cakes lighter.

GLOSSARY

BRITISH	AMERICAN
Aubergines	Eggplants
Baking Beans	Used with Waxed Paper to line a Pie Crust to prevent it rising in baking. Use large beans, such as Lima Beans
Baking Blind	To cook a Pie Shell
Balloon Whisk	Egg Beater
Batter	Dough or Mixture
Bicarbonate of Soda	Baking Soda
Bread Tins	Bread Pans
Broad Beans	Fava Beans
Butter Beans	Lima Beans
Cake Mixture	Cake Batter
Cake Tins	Cake Pans
Chick Peas	Gabanzos Beans
Cling Film	Plastic Wrap
Courgette	Zucchini
Crisps	Potato Chips
Crystallized Ginger	Candied Ginger
Digestive Biscuits	Graham Crackers
Fish Slice	Spatula
Flan Case	Pie Shell
Fresh Yeast or Dried Yeast	Compressed Yeast or Active Dry Yeast
Frying Pan	Skillet
Gluhwein	Germanic – Hot Mulled Wine
Greaseproof Paper	Waxed Paper
Haricot Beans	Navy Beans
Jug	Pitcher
Kitchen Roll	Paper Towel
Mangetout	Snow Peas
Pepper, Red or Green Sweet	Capsicum
Plain Flour	All Purpose Flour
Pudding Basin	Ovenproof Basin
Rissole	Burger Shaped Savory
Runner Beans	String or Pole Beans
Sandwich Tins	Cake Tins
Single Cream	Coffee Cream
Spring Onions	Scallions
Sugar, Dark Muscovado	Dark Raw Sugar
Sugar, Demerara	Raw Cane Sugar
Sugar, Icing	Confectioner's Sugar
Sugar, Light Muscovado	Light Raw Sugar
Sultanas	Seedless White Raisins
Swede	Rutabaga
Swiss Roll	Jelly Roll
Unbaked Pastry Case	Unbaked Pie Shell
Vegan	Vegetarian who also will not eat any product from animals, milk, eggs, honey, nor do they wear clothes made from any animal product.
Vegetable Marrow	Squash/Large Zucchini

JANUARY

In our house, January was the month we made marmalade. My mother and grandmother are great fans of the humble Seville orange. I cannot remember a year go by without my mum turning her kitchen into a mini marmalade factory. The smell as it cooked invited you to sit and devour a chunk of bread spread with a thick layer of freshly made preserve. A couple of sessions in the kitchen can produce enough marmalade to keep the average family going all year.

If you find it impossible to complete the making in one day, freeze the cooked fruit before the sugar is added. Make careful note of quantities on the container. You can then take it out and continue when it is more convenient. As well as a selection of marmalade recipes, I have included a section on how to test for the setting point, and how to bottle preserves. And I show how easy it is to make the bread to spread your marmalade on!

As the weather can be rather inclement in January, it is sensible to make use of any dry days we do have by doing maintenance work in the garden.

As well as general tidying up, walls can be built and paths relaid. Now is a good time to construct a compost bin. Get into the habit of collecting scraps for the compost. Brussel sprout stalks can be crushed with a hammer and thrown on. Burn the roots if there is any sign of club root. Don't add the open Brussel sprouts, though, they can be used to make soup (page 22). Nothing need ever be wasted.

Those who have previously planted their gardens will have quite a few crops available. Brussel sprouts are in abundance. There are also leeks, cabbage, swedes, parsnips and kale. You may have stored potatoes, carrots, onions and beetroot. Using these tasty vegetables, we can make a great variety of delicious meals that will provide warmth and sustenance during cold January days.

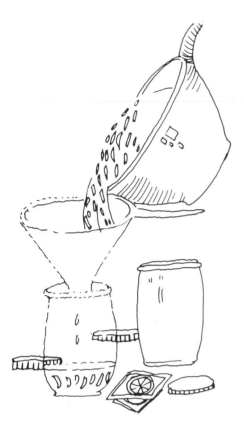

MARMALADE AND JAM MAKING

Making preserves is the perfect seasonal activity. January is my month for marmalade; make the most of rhubarb crops in April (page 57); cheap strawberries and raspberries in July (page 92) and hedgerow fruits in October (page 128).

I have used raw cane Demerara sugar throughout the preserves recipes – I like the result it gives. I find Muscovado sugar too strong in taste. Warming the sugar first in a bowl in the oven hastens the dissolving and allows the preserve to reach setting point more quickly. You can use a food processor to chop the fruit – it may make the preserve a little cloudy but will not affect the flavour.

Making marmalade and jam is easier if you have a heavy-based pan. This minimizes the risk of burning the preserve when you are boiling it to reach setting point. A sugar thermometer is handy, but not essential – you can wrinkle test on a saucer (see below).

Tests for the Setting Point

If you have a sugar thermometer, warm it and lower it into the preserve after 20 to 30 minutes' boiling. If the preserve has reached setting point, the thermometer will register 220°F / 105°C.

Alternatively, use 'the wrinkle test'. Spoon a little boiling preserve on a saucer. Let it cool slightly, then push the surface with a fingertip. If there is a skin there that wrinkles, the preserve has reached setting point.

Bottling Preserves

Jars for bottling should be sterilized: wash them thoroughly, then place them in a warm oven to get completely dry and heated through. Use them while they are still hot.

A bottling funnel makes it easier to pour the preserve into the jars, but a cup or ladle is perfectly adequate. Fill the jars to about 1 cm (½ inch) of the rims.

Proper sealing is important to inhibit mould growth. Buy jam-pot cover kits from stationers – these contain all you need. Put a waxed disc directly onto the preserve. Moisten one side of a cellophane cover then stretch it – wet side up – over the jar and secure it with a rubber band. Don't forget to label the jars!

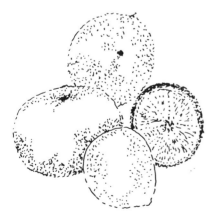

Ronaldson's Scotch Marmalade

This recipe brings back memories from my childhood when, during the school holidays, I used to stay with my grandparents at their smallholding. My grandmother used to have a larder which had rows of jewel-coloured jams and marmalades filling the shelves. My grandfather was a Scot, hence the popularity of this recipe. It makes about 6 lb / 3 kg.

8 Seville oranges
2 large lemons
6 pints / 4 litres / 15 cups water
6 lb / 3 kg / 16 cups Demerara sugar
1 tbsp molasses
4 tbsp whisky

Prepare the fruit and cook as for *3 Fruit Marmalade*, adding the molasses with the sugar. Stir in the whisky once the setting point has been reached. Stir and leave to absorb. Bottle and seal.

3 Fruit Marmalade

This makes about 6 lb / 3 kg.

3 lb / 1.5 kg / 8 cups fruit (2 grapefruit, 3 sweet oranges, make up to 3 lb with lemons)
6 pints / 4 litres / 15 cups water
6 lb / 3 kg / 16 cups sugar

Thoroughly scrub the fruit, cut into halves and squeeze out the juice into a large pan. Scrape some of the pith and membrane away from the peel and tie this into a little muslin bag along with the pips. Cut the peel into the desired thickness and put into the pan with the water. Tie the muslin bag onto the handle of the pan and put in with the fruit. Bring to the boil, reduce heat and simmer for about 2 hours until the fruit is tender enough to disintegrate when squeezed between the fingers. (If the fruit is not cooked sufficiently before the sugar is added, it will make the fruit tough.)

Remove the muslin bag and squeeze the juice from it into the pan. Add the sugar which will dissolve more quickly if it has been warmed in the oven first. Stir the marmalade over a low heat until the sugar dissolves. Bring to the boil and continue to boil until setting point is reached. This will take between 20 and 30 minutes. Bottle the marmalade (opposite page).

Grapefruit and Ginger Marmalade

This makes about 5 lb / 2.5 kg.

3 grapefruit
3 lemons
4 pints / 2.5 litres / 10 cups water
8 oz / 225 g / 1 cup stem ginger
3 lb / 1.5 kg / 8 cups Demerara sugar

Peel the grapefruit and lemons with a potato peeler and cut the peel into desired sizes. Continue as for *3 Fruit Marmalade*, adding the chopped ginger with the sugar.

Pineapple Marmalade

This makes about 5 lb / 2.5 kg.

2 medium-sized sweet oranges
2 or 3 lemons (make the weight up to
1¼lb / 625 g with the oranges)
13 oz / 375 g / 2 cups canned pineapple in its
   own juice
1 small lime
2 pints / 1.25 litres / 5 cups water
3 lb / 1.5 kg / 8 cups sugar
1 teaspoon butter

Scrub and peel the fruit and cut the peel up very finely. Put the pith and seeds into a muslin bag. Put the fruit into a large pan with the water. Bring to the boil and add the sugar. Simmer until dissolved. Bring back to the boil until setting point is reached, add the butter at the end of cooking to prevent scum forming. Allow to cool for about 10 minutes to allow fruit to settle. Bottle and seal (page 16).

Pineapple Tart

Use the Pineapple Marmalade for this recipe to make a delicious dessert.

Use an 8 inch (20 cm) pre-baked wholemeal pastry case. Fill it with marmalade and sprinkle the top with desiccated coconut. Bake for 20 to 25 minutes in a 375°F / 190°C / Mark 6 oven. Serve hot or cold.

BREADMAKING

January is a good month to resolve to tackle the task of making your own bread. There seems to be some mystique surrounding cooking with yeast, but it is really very simple. I have had five-year-olds make bread without much trouble. It is a very rewarding task, and there is nothing to beat the aroma of freshly baked bread as it pervades the whole house.

Bread dough is very amenable stuff – the more you prod and poke the better it is. The only thing it does not like is the heat. This kills the yeast and stops it rising. So be careful never to have the liquid too hot. Having it too cold will only mean the rising time will be longer.

You can experiment with all types of ingredients in your bread for texture and flavour, and with all the different types of wholemeal flour available.

I always used to let my bread have two risings until I went to work in the Cranks bakery in Dartmouth where I was introduced to the one-rise method. I was surprised how much more flavour it gave the bread, although the texture is a lot heavier.

Basic Wholemeal Bread

Pour the flour and salt into a large bowl. Run your fingers through the flour to incorporate some air (you can sieve the flour if you wish). If you are using the easybake yeast, mix this into the flour. You can add the fresh yeast directly too, or you can mix it in a small bowl with the molasses or honey. Add a little liquid and allow it to froth up about 2 cm (¾ inch). Make a well in the centre of the flour and pour in the yeast and remaining liquid. Knead thoroughly in the bowl, then add the margarine. When it is well mixed, place the dough on a worktop and knead until it is smooth and elastic. Cut it into desired sizes and either place in loaf tins which have been well greased or shape into plaited loaves etc. Leave to rise until double in size. I place my bread inside a large greased plastic bag and tie the end to let it incubate.

Do be careful not to let the dough rise too much, or you will find that the crust will fly away from the bread when it is cooking. If you find the bread is ready to go into the oven but the oven is full, knock the bread back and reknead. You can allow your bread to rise overnight in the refrigerator and cook it fresh in the morning for breakfast.

It is possible to freeze uncooked dough. Flatten the dough like a pancake and it will defrost more easily. Place in a plastic bag and freeze. When needed, allow to defrost and continue as for fresh bread.

Bake the bread in a preheated oven at 425°F / 210°C / Mark 7 for 5 minutes to kill the yeast, then reduce the heat to 400°F / 200°C / Mark 6 for about 40 minutes. The bread will sound hollow when tapped on the bottom if it is cooked. Use this method to make all types of bread.

There are many different types of flour to try although some are low in gluten which is the substance in the flour which helps it rise. Adding 1 part Soya flour to 7 parts wholemeal adds protein. Millet flakes, oat flakes, sunflower seeds, sesame seeds, chopped nuts are all things which can be added. Try using poppy seed as a decorative topping. Cracked wheat is another attractive decoration. For something more unusual, try caraway, cumin or aniseed. Use some sugar dissolved in hot water brushed on top of the loaves to get seeds to stick.

3.3 lb / 1½ kg / 13 cups wholemeal flour

2 oz / 60 g / 2 cakes compressed fresh yeast or 1 oz / 30 g / 2 tbsp dried yeast (the easybake variety is good as it is very quick acting)

1 oz / 50 g / 3 tsp fine sea salt

1 tbsp molasses *or* 1 tbsp honey (this also helps the cutting quality of the bread)

1 oz / 30 g / 2 tbsp vegetable margarine (this is optional but it gives the bread a better cutting quality)

1¾ pints / 1 litre / 4 cups tepid water. (You can use a mixture of milk and water if preferred. The amount of liquid needed can alter with different types of flour so you will have to adjust accordingly. The dough continues to soak up moisture while resting so add water until the dough is just slightly sticky.)

19

Granary Bread

3 lb / 1½ kg / 13 cups Granary Meal
2 oz / 60 g / 2 cakes compressed fresh yeast
1¼ pints / ¾ litre / 3 cups tepid water
1 tbsp malt extract
1 oz / 50 g / 3 teaspoons fine sea salt

Use the method as for Basic Wholemeal Bread. Knead thoroughly. Place into baking tins, cover and allow to rise. Bake in a preheated oven at 425°F / 200°C / Mark 7 for 45 – 50 minutes.

Wholemeal Croissants

This recipe will make 12 croissants.

1 lb / 500 g / 4 cups wholemeal flour
1 oz / 25 g / 1 cake compressed fresh yeast
1 tsp honey
1 pint / 600 ml / 2½ cups milk and water
    mixed
pinch salt
8 oz / 250 g / 1 cup butter (margarine just
    does not taste the same)

Mix the honey with the yeast and a little of the tepid milk. Allow to froth. Mix the salt into the flour. Mix the yeast into the flour, add the remaining liquid and mix until you have a smooth dough. Cover and leave in a warm place to double in size.

Knead the dough lightly and roll it out into an oblong shape. Divide the butter into three. Dot one part over the dough covering ⅔ of the surface – keep slightly away from the edges. Fold the unbuttered section of dough over the middle, then fold the other section over this. Seal the edges with a rolling pin. Place the dough in refrigerator for ½ hour. Roll out the dough and repeat the folding process twice more with the remaining butter. Allow to rest once more. On a floured board roll out the dough into a rectangle. Cut the dough into 12 triangles 9 x 9 inches / 23 x 23 cm with a 6 inch / 15 cm base. Roll the croissants from the base and curl them around into crescent shapes. Place on a baking sheet and allow to rise once more. Brush with a beaten egg and bake in a preheated oven at 425°F / 220°C / Mark 7 for about 15 minutes until golden and well risen.

Chelsea Buns

Use half the ingredients as for Basic Wholemeal Bread (page 19). Continue until you get to the raising stage. Roll the dough into a rectangle.

Melt the butter, allow to cool then spread over the dough. Mix the spices and sugar into the fruit and then sprinkle that on the dough. Roll up into a long Swiss roll shape. Cut into 2.5 cm (1 inch) slices and place on a greased baking sheet.

Cover the slices and allow to rise to double the size. Bake in a preheated oven at 425°F / 220°C / Mark 7 for 15 minutes. While the buns cook, make the glaze by boiling the sugar and water together to form a syrup. Remove the buns from the oven and cool on a wire rack. Brush with the glaze.

4 oz / 125 g / ½ cup margarine or butter
8 oz / 250 g / 1¼ cups currants and raisins, mixed
1 tsp mixed spice
1 tsp ground cinnamon
3 oz / 75 g / ½ cup sugar

Glaze
⅙ pint / 100 ml / ⅓ cup water
1 heaped tsp Demerara sugar

Orange and Nut Buns

These little buns, full of flavour, are absolutely delicious.

Mix the salt with the flour. Mix the yeast with a little of the milk and allow to froth. Melt the butter in the remaining milk, then stir in the sugar. Pour the sultanas, orange rind and juice and orange oil into the milk. Allow to cool until hand hot and then stir into the flour, with the yeast mixture and egg. Mix in the pine kernels. Knead the dough thoroughly, cover and allow to rise. Break into 6 pieces, place on a baking tray and allow to rise once again. Brush with the egg and milk glaze. Bake in a preheated oven at 400°F / 200°C / Mark 6 for 20–25 minutes. Cool on a wire rack. Make the glaze by boiling the sugar and water together, and brush this over the buns.

12 oz / 375 g / 3 cups plain strong white unbleached flour
pinch salt
10 g / 1 tsp fresh yeast
¼ pint / 150 ml / ⅔ cup milk
2 oz / 50 g / ¼ cup butter
2 oz / 50 g / ⅓ cup light Muscovado sugar
3 oz / 75 g / ⅓ cup sultanas
finely grated rind and juice 2 oranges
couple drops orange oil
1 egg, beaten
3 tbsp roughly chopped pine kernels (pignolia nuts)
1 egg and little milk to glaze

Glaze
⅙ pint / 100 ml / ⅓ cup water
1 heaped tsp Demerara sugar

Brussel Sprout Soup

For this soup you can use sprouts that have opened.

12 oz / 350 g / 3 cups Brussel sprouts
1 large onion, chopped
10 oz / 350 g / 1⅔ cups peeled potatoes
1¾ pints / 1 litre / 4½ cups vegetable stock
freshly ground salt and pepper to taste

Heat a little oil in a large pan and gently fry the onion for about 5 minutes until soft, but not brown. Dice the potatoes and add to the pan with the stock. Bring to the boil and then reduce the heat and simmer for 15 minutes until the potatoes are just tender. Thoroughly wash the sprouts and add to the pan, then continue to cook for a further 15 minutes. Allow to cool slightly and then liquidize. Return the soup to the pan and season. Reheat to serve.

Leek and Coriander Soup

Leeks are inexpensive and plentiful and a good base for a truly tasty soup.

1½ lb / 675 g/ 4 cups leeks
2 tsp crushed coriander seeds
4 oz / 125 g / ½ cup margarine
3 medium carrots (scrubbed but not peeled)
4 medium potatoes (scrubbed but not peeled)
2½ pints / 1.5 litres / 6¼ cups vegetable stock
salt and pepper to taste

Melt the margarine in a large pan. Fry the coriander seeds for a few minutes to release their flavour. Add the leeks and carrots to the pan and cook until the leeks are soft – about 10 minutes. Add the potatoes and stock. Bring to the boil, reduce the heat, and simmer for 30 minutes until the vegetables are soft. Remove a few pieces of leek for texture, then liquidize the remaining soup. Season and replace the leek pieces. Reheat to serve, garnished with croutons.

Bean Casserole

Soak the three types of bean separately overnight in cold water. Drain and rinse them in the morning. Put the soya and butter beans together in a pan of cold water, bring to the boil, then simmer for an hour. In another pan of water, bring the red kidney beans to the boil. Boil for 10 minutes, then reduce the heat and continue to simmer for ½ hour. Remove the beans from the heat, drain, and pour into a large casserole dish.

In a pan with a little oil, slightly soften the celery and onion. Mix these into the dish with the beans, then stir in all the other ingredients. Bake in a 350°F / 180°C / Mark 3 oven for between 2½ and 3 hours until the casserole is thickened and the beans are soft. While it is baking, check occasionally to make sure there is enough liquid in the dish, adding more stock if necessary.

8 oz / 250 g / 1⅓ cups soya beans
8 oz / 250 g / 1⅓ cups red kidney beans
8 oz / 250 g / 1⅓ cups butter beans
6 sticks celery
3 large onions, chopped
2 pints / 1¼ litres / 5 cups vegetable stock
2 tsp vegetable extract
2 tsp dried mixed herbs
14 oz / 400 g / 2 cups canned tomatoes
1 tbsp tomato purée
½ tsp French mustard

Lentil and Mushroom Roast

Grease a 12 x 8 x 5 inch (30 × 20 × 12 cm) baking tin. Rinse the lentils thoroughly in running cold water, then simmer them in the water for 15 minutes until soft. Fry the onion in a little oil until it is transparent. Add the mushrooms and cook gently until soft. Mix the tomato purée into the lentils, then stir in the egg, breadcrumbs, herbs and lemon juice. Season and mix in most of the cheese, reserving a little to sprinkle on the top. Spread half the lentil mix into the baking tin and cover it with the onion and mushroom mixture. Spread the remaining lentils on top of this. Then sprinkle on the remaining cheese. Bake for 30 minutes at 375°F / 190°C / Mark 6 until golden brown. Serve with a tasty sauce, such as the Peanut Sauce on page 33.

12 oz / 375 g / 2 cups red lentils
1 pint / 60 cl / 2½ cups water
1 medium onion, finely chopped
6 oz / 175 g / 1½ cups finely sliced mushrooms
1 tbsp tomato purée
1 beaten egg
3 oz / 90 g / 1½ cups wholemeal bread-crumbs
1 tsp dried mixed herbs
1 tbsp lemon juice
salt and pepper to taste
6 oz / 175 g / 1½ cups grated Cheddar cheese

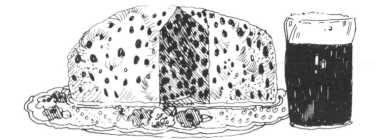

Old Fashioned Stout Cake

A simple cake to make, with a good keeping quality.

8 oz / 250 g / 1 cup vegetable margarine
6 oz / 150 g / 1 cup medium Muscovado sugar
1¼ lb / 625 g / 3¼ cups mixed cake fruit
1 tbsp molasses
12 fl oz / 300 ml / 1¼ cups stout
12 oz / 375 g / 3 cups 100% plain wholemeal flour
2 tsp mixed spice
4 eggs, beaten
4 oz / 125 g / 1 cup walnut pieces

Simmer the margarine, sugar, fruit, molasses and stout for 20 minutes. Leave to cool and then add to the sifted flour and spices in a large mixing bowl with the eggs and walnut pieces. Pour into a greased and lined 8 inch (20 cm) cake tin. Bake at 300°F / 150°C / Mark 2 for 2 hours until cooked. If in doubt, test with a skewer – it should come out clean. Leave the cake to cool in the tin for 10 minutes before turning out onto a wire rack.

Victoria Sandwich

4 oz / 125 g / 1 cup 85% self-raising flour
4 oz / 125 g / ⅔ cup light Muscovado sugar
4 oz / 125 g / ½ cup vegetable margarine
3 medium eggs
drop of real vanilla essence

This is a sponge cake using the creaming method, as it contains a high proportion of fat. You can make a very good Victoria Sandwich using 85% stoneground flour. This means the heaviest part of the flour has been sifted out. You can use 100% self-raising flour but the result will be a little close textured.

Sift the flour. Cream the sugar and margarine until light and fluffy. Gradually add the eggs, beating well. Sift in a little flour to prevent curdling. Add the vanilla essence. Fold in the remaining flour. Divide the mixture between two 7 inch (18 cm) sandwich cake tins. Bake in a preheated oven at 350°F / 180°C / Mark 4 for 20–25 minutes until golden brown or the cake springs back when pressed with a fingertip. Allow to cool slightly in the tins. Turn onto a wire rack and allow to cool completely. Use jam or cream, or both, to sandwich the sponge together.

HOME REMEDIES FOR COLDS

At this time of year, many people feel under par. When the body is in a low state it is more susceptible to germs – colds and 'flu especially.

Here are a few simple home treatments to use to alleviate the symptoms. They do not cure. Your body does that in its own good time. The best way of preventing colds and 'flu is to raise the standard of your general health. Aim to change your habits of diet and exercise.

There are a number of patent remedies you can buy at health stores. Olbas Oil is great for many different uses; you can rub it on chests, inhale it to unblock stuffy noses, gargle with it for a sore throat, even rub it on aches and pains. For 'flu-type colds, try something with elderflower, peppermint and capsicum in it. Taking a course of garlic capsules is a good way of building up resistance to germs.

An old remedy for colds and 'flu is to sprinkle a raw onion with sugar, leave for about an hour and drink the resulting liquid. Or try eating a whole baked onion before retiring for the night. A mustard bath is a great relief. Put a tablespoon of dry mustard powder into a bowl of water as hot as you can stand, and then immerse your feet for 15 minutes or so.

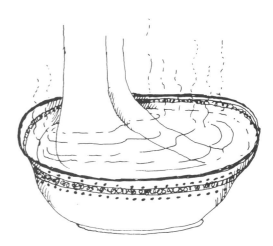

Red Sage Tea *(Salvia officinalis)*

Sore throats can be helped by gargling with this tea.
   Take 1 oz / 30 g / ½ cup sage leaves and pour 1 pint / 60 cl / 2½ cups of boiling water over them. Allow to steep for at least 5 minutes. Strain it into a jug or pitcher. Add 2 or 3 teaspoons of honey, give it a good stir and use as a gargle three times daily. You can also drink the mixture if you prefer. This should not be used excessively.

Lemon Barley Water

This is a nourishing and soothing drink to give to convalescents.
   Wash the barley thoroughly in several changes of water. This will rid it of husks and dust. Tie the lemon peels in a piece of muslin with any seeds and tie onto the handle of a large saucepan. Pour the water into the saucepan. Add the barley and boil for 1 hour. Add the lemon juice, then sweeten to taste.

3 tbsp pearl barley
2 lemons with the juice extracted
2 pints / 1.25 litres / 5 cups water
sugar or honey to taste

FEBRUARY

February is still apt to be dark and wet sometimes, so it's lovely for children arriving home from school to find a welcoming teatime snack waiting. If you are working, this is still possible with the aid of freezer and microwave. Set aside an occasional day off to fill the freezer with goodies such as the Carrot and Hazelnut Cake (page 35) and tasty soups (page 30) that can be quickly defrosted to provide a warming supper on a bleak February evening.

February brings us Shrove Tuesday – pancake day. As a change from lemon and sugar, there are plenty of different savoury or sweet fillings for a substantial supper dish. Try the Cauliflower Cheese with Walnuts (page 31), or the Tofu and Apricot (page 29) if you have a sweet tooth. As it is also St. Valentine's Day this month, there is a special heartshaped passion cake for you to make for your sweetheart.

Vegetables are plentiful this month. Turnips, parsnips, swedes, cabbage, curly kale, leeks, onions, carrots and potatoes are all readily available in the shops if you have not supplies from the garden, making the basis of a wide variety of winter vegetarian dishes.

It is probably still too cold to plant the garden, but you can start to plan where you are going to plant everything. Sow vegetables in boxes ready to be planted out in March – cauliflower, cabbage, lettuce, peas and broad beans can all be started off this way. Strawberries can be planted this month, although August is the preferred time to plant. Early potatoes should be put in during the last week of this month.

It is a good idea to buy yourself a diary or notebook so you can keep track of your work. You need to work on a rotation system using four beds for different crops in order to prevent the build up of disease.

Pancakes

8 oz / 250 g / 2 cups plain wholemeal flour
pinch salt
1 egg
½ pint / ¼ litre / 1¼ cups milk

Sift the flour, add the salt, and mix them together. Make a well in the centre of the flour and break the egg into it. Beat well until smooth, gradually adding the milk. Heat a little oil in a frying pan until it is really hot. Pour in just enough batter to cover the bottom thinly and cook the pancake until golden brown. Turn the pancake over and cook the other side. You can precook them and stack them in between layers of greaseproof paper and either freeze or refrigerate.

Buckwheat Pancakes

4 oz / 100 g / 1 cup buckwheat flour
1 oz / 25 g / ¼ cup soya flour
1 egg
¼ pint / 150 ml / ⅔ cup mixture of milk and
    water
pinch salt
1 tbsp vegetable oil

Buckwheat has a very distinctive flavour particularly suitable for savoury pancakes.

Beat all the ingredients together in a bowl. Buckwheat soaks up a lot of liquid so it is a good idea to let the batter stand for a little while – then, if it seems a bit too thick, add more milk and water. Cook as for Pancakes, above.

Pancake Fillings

There are countless pancake fillings besides the traditional lemon and sugar. Either spread the fillings on to the pancakes and roll or fold them to serve; or serve the fillings as a condiment so everyone can help themselves.

Lemon Curd and Curd Cheese

Whip together 4 oz / 125 g / ½ cup low fat curd cheese and 3 tbsp lemon curd.

This is also delicious in a Victoria Sandwich cake (recipe on page 24).

Spiced Apple

Mix all the ingredients together and heat through before serving with the pancakes.

1 lb / 500 g / 2 cups stewed apple
2 oz / 50 g / ¼ cup sultanas
¼ tspn ground cinnamon

Pear and Honey Sauce

Combine all the ingredients together and cook gently until the pears are soft.

3 pears, diced and cored
4 tsp clear honey
1 tsp lemon juice
1 tsp margarine
pinch cinnamon

Tofu and Apricot

Cook the apricots in a little water. When soft, add the chopped tofu. Fill the pancakes, sprinkle them with nuts and then dribble the maple syrup over the top.

4 oz / 100 g / ⅔ cup dried apricots
3 oz / 75 g / ½ cup tofu, diced
1 oz / 25 g / ¼ cup chopped pecan nuts
1 tbsp maple syrup

Vegetable Mulligatawny Soup

4 oz / 100 g / ½ cup margarine
2 carrots, scrubbed and diced
2 small leeks, washed and shredded
1 turnip, scrubbed and diced
4 oz / 125 g / 1 cup chopped celery
2 pints / 1¼ litres /5 cups vegetable stock
4 tbsp cooked haricot beans
2 shallots, finely chopped
1 small apple, chopped
2 tbsp wholemeal flour
3 tsp curry powder
1 oz / 25 g / 1 tablespoon sultanas
juice of 1 lemon
salt
1 bay leaf

Melt a quarter of the margarine and sauté all the vegetables except for the shallots for about 8 minutes, until just brown. Add half of the stock and continue to cook until the vegetables are tender. Take the pan from the heat and drop in the cooked beans. Fry the shallots and apple in the remaining margarine for 3 minutes. Stir in the flour, curry powder, sultanas and lemon juice and cook for 2 minutes. Add salt and the bay leaf. Mix this in with the vegetables and beans. Pour in the remaining stock and simmer for another 20 minutes, then serve.

Cauliflower Soup

1 small cauliflower, divided into sprigs
1 onion, peeled and finely chopped
1 oz / 25 g / 2 tablespoons margarine
1 oz / 25 g / ¼ cup plain wholemeal flour
¾ pint / ½ litre / 2 cups mild vegetable
   stock
a little grated nutmeg
salt and pepper to taste
1 tsp cayenne pepper
¾ pint / ½ litre / 2 cups milk

In a pan, sauté the cauliflower sprigs and onion in the margarine for about 5 minutes or until the onion is transparent. Stir in the flour and cook for a further 5 minutes. Gradually stir in the vegetable stock and then place a lid on the pan and allow to cook for another ¼ hour or until the vegetables are fairly soft. Remove the pan from the heat and allow the soup to cool before putting it through a blender – first reserving a few of the vegetable pieces to add texture. Return the soup and vegetable pieces to the pan and add the seasoning. Slowly stir in the milk as the soup is reheating.

Cauliflower Cheese with Walnuts

This is delicious on its own or as a stuffing for pancake rolls (see below).

Trim the cauliflower and cook it whole in boiling salted water for 12 minutes. It has to be fairly crisp. Drain the cauliflower and cut it in half, then place in an ovenproof dish. Keep it warm while you prepare the sauce.

Melt the margarine, then add the mustard, salt and pepper. Add the flour and cook for 3 minutes. Gradually add the milk, stirring all the time to make sure that the sauce does not go lumpy. Add most of the cheese, reserving a little to sprinkle on the top. Stir in most of the walnuts, reserving a few of them also to put on the top. Pour the sauce over the cauliflower. Sprinkle on the reserved cheese and put under a hot grill for about 5 minutes to brown. Serve immediately.

1 large cauliflower
3 oz / 75 g / ⅓ cup margarine
1 tsp prepared English mustard
salt and pepper
3 oz / 75 g / ¾ cup flour
¾ pint / 450 ml / 2 cups milk
6 oz / 150 g / ¾ cup Cheddar cheese
3 oz / 75 g / ¾ cup chopped walnuts

Stuffed Pancakes

Make some buckwheat pancakes (page 28). Prepare Cauliflower Cheese with Walnuts (above), reserving a little cheese sauce to pour over the top of the pancakes.

Put a large spoonful of cauliflower cheese into the middle of each pancake. Fold in the ends, roll up, and place in an ovenproof dish. Pour the cheese sauce over the top, and sprinkle with grated Cheddar cheese. Bake for 20 minutes at 375°F / 190°C / Mark 5 until golden brown.

Buckwheat and Peanut Roast

8 oz / 250 g / 1 cup long-grain brown rice
8 oz / 250 g / 1⅓ cup unroasted buckwheat
½ pint / ¼ litre / 1⅓ cup boiling water
1 large onion, finely chopped
8 oz / 250 g / 4 cups finely chopped
    mushrooms
4 tbsp crunchy peanut butter
3 tbsp chopped fresh parsley
salt and pepper to taste

Cook the rice (page 135). Heat a little oil in another pan and fry the buckwheat for 4 minutes. When it is brown, add the water and simmer for 20 minutes until soft. Heat a little oil in a third pan and lightly fry the onion, add the mushrooms and cook until soft. Drain the rice and buckwheat and combine all the ingredients together. Grease a large 3 lb (1.5 kg) loaf tin and press the mixture into it. Bake for 45–50 minutes at 350°F / 180°C / Mark 4. Serve hot or cold with Peanut Sauce (page 33).

Boston Baked Beans

1 lb / 500 g / 2 cups Haricot beans
1 onion, finely chopped
2 cloves garlic, crushed
1½ tsp dark Muscovado sugar
3 tbsp molasses
½ tbsp dried English Mustard
1 tsp salt
2 tbsp tomato purée

A hearty dish on a cold winter's day or very good for a midsummer barbecue. These beans cook brilliantly in a Slow Cooker.

Put the beans in a saucepan and cover with water. Bring to the boil, reduce the heat and cook for 20 minutes. Remove the beans from the heat and leave to stand for an hour, then drain the water off. Pour the beans into a large casserole dish and mix in all the other ingredients. Pour enough hot water over the beans to cover. Bake for 4 hours at 250°F / 100°C / Mark 1. Check occasionally during the cooking time to make sure the beans are not drying out. Add more water where necessary. Serve with vegetables and crusty bread for a substantial meal.

Cheese and Potato Pie

Put the milk in a saucepan with the peppercorns, parsley and bay leaf and bring to the boil, then reduce the heat to a simmer and cook for 5 minutes. Strain the milk.

Melt the margarine in a saucepan, then add the flour and cook for 2 minutes. Gradually add the milk, stirring thoroughly to prevent lumps from forming. Stir the sauce into the mashed potato, adding ¾ of the cheese as well. Season it with salt and pepper and transfer to a baking dish. Sprinkle the pie with the remaining cheese and bake for 30 minutes at 375°F / 190°C / Mark 5.

½ pint / ¼ litre / 1⅓ cup milk
6 peppercorns
3 sprigs parsley
1 bay leaf
2 oz / 60 g / ¼ cup margarine
2 oz / 60 g / ½ cup plain flour
1½ lb / 750 g / 5 cups potatoes, cooked and mashed with 1 egg
8 oz / 250 g / 2 cups grated cheese

Nut Steaks

Lightly fry the onion. Mix all the other ingredients together in a large bowl. Stir in the onion and leave to stand for about an hour so all the moisture is absorbed. Shape into 6 steaks, coat with egg and roll in the breadcrumbs. Fry in a little oil until golden brown. Drain on some kitchen towels.

1 medium onion, finely chopped
4 oz / 125 g / 1 cup ground hazelnuts
2 oz / 60 g / ½ cup ground peanuts
2 oz / 60 g / ½ cup ground sunflower seeds
1 egg
4 tbsp milk
2 tbsp soya flour
1½ tsp shoyu
dash of tabasco sauce
½ tsp dried sage
½ tsp dried thyme
salt and freshly ground pepper to taste

Coating
1 egg
4 oz / 125 g / 2 cups wholemeal breadcrumbs

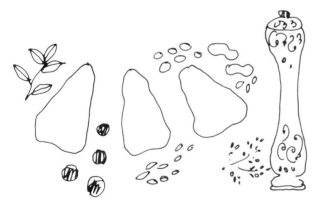

Peanut Sauce

Fry the onion in a little oil until transparent. Add the green pepper and continue to cook until soft. Stir in the peanut butter, tomatoes and tomato purée. Continue to simmer for about 10 minutes, adding enough of the stock to make a thick sauce. Season to taste.

1 small onion, finely chopped
½ green pepper, finely diced
4 tbsp smooth peanut butter
14 oz / 400 g / 2 cups canned tomatoes
1 tsp tomato purée
4 tbsp vegetable stock
salt and pepper to taste

Passion Cake

6 oz / 165 g / ¾ cup margarine
6 oz / 165 g / 1 cup light Muscovado sugar
3 large eggs
8 oz / 250 g / 2 cups 85% self-raising flour
2 oz / 50 g / ½ cup chopped walnuts
2 medium carrots, finely grated
2 large ripe bananas, mashed
1 tsp ground cinnamon
approximately 2 tbsp milk

Filling and Topping
12 oz / 375 g / 1½ cups low-fat soft cream
  cheese
1 tsp lemon juice
2 oz / 50 g / ⅓ cup light Muscovado sugar,
  liquidized to icing sugar
2 bananas, mashed
1 oz / 25 g / ¼ cup finely chopped walnuts
few whole walnuts for decoration

Set the oven to 325°F / 160°C / Mark 3. Grease and line an 8 inch (20 cm) cake tin. Use one in the shape of a heart if you want to be romantic! (The cooking time may differ slightly.)

Mix the margarine and sugar together until pale and fluffy. Beat the eggs in one at a time, adding a little flour to prevent curdling. Stir in the remaining flour, nuts, carrots, banana and cinnamon. Mix thoroughly, and add a little of the milk if the mixture seems too stiff. Pour into the baking tin and cook for 1–1¼ hours until the cake is golden brown and has shrunk slightly from the side of the tin. It should spring back when pressed with a finger.

Prepare the filling by mixing all the ingredients together in a bowl. When the cake is thoroughly cooled, cut it across the middle and sandwich it together, with some of the filling. Coat the sides with filling and finally swirl it on to the top. Decorate with the whole walnuts.

Carrot and Hazelnut Cake

This is a lovely moist cake.

Grease and line a 7 × 5 × 3 inch (18 × 12 × 8 cm) baking tin. Preheat the oven to 325°F / 170°C / Mark 3.

Cream the margarine and sugar until light and fluffy. Gradually beat the egg yolks into the mixture. In a separate bowl, whisk the egg whites until stiff. Sift the flour, cinnamon and baking powder together in a bowl. Stir the flour mixture into the margarine mixture along with the carrots and hazelnuts. Cut the egg whites gently into the mixture so that they do not lose the air bubbles. Pour into the prepared cake tin and bake for 1½ hours, reducing the heat to 275°F / 140°C / Mark 1 for a further 20 minutes. Do check occasionally during the last 20 minutes in case the cake is already cooked. Test it by inserting a skewer which should come out cleanly.

6 oz / 165 g / ¾ cup margarine
6 oz / 165 g / 1 cup medium Muscovado sugar
3 eggs, separated
8 oz / 250 g / 2 cups plain wholemeal flour
1 tsp ground cinnamon
2 tsp baking powder
8 oz / 250 g / 1½ cups finely grated carrots
4 oz / 125 g / 1 cup finely chopped hazelnuts

St. Clement's Cheesecake

For the base, melt the margarine and then stir in the biscuits, sugar and cinnamon. Press into the base of a lined 8 inch (20 cm) diameter loose-bottom cake tin. Bake for 20 minutes at 350°F / 180°C / Mark 4. Watch it does not burn around the edges – lower the temperature if need be.

Whisk the egg whites until very stiff. Mix all the other ingredients together in a bowl. Gently fold in the egg white. Pour on to the base and bake for 35–45 minutes or until it has set. Allow to cool and then decorate with the slices of orange.

Base
3 oz / 75 g / ¾ cup margarine or butter
6 oz / 165 g / 3 cups digestive biscuits, crushed
2 oz / 50 g / ⅓ cup light Muscovado sugar
pinch cinnamon

Topping
2 eggs, separated
1 lb / 500 g / 2 cups soft low-fat cream cheese
3 tbsp orange juice
2 tbsp lemon juice
finely grated rind 1 lemon and 1 orange
2 oz / 50 g / ⅓ cup light Muscovado sugar
¼ tsp vanilla extract
slices of orange for decoration

Keeping Free-Range Chickens

With Spring just around the corner, lighter evenings and better weather, why not give some thought to rearing chickens. The flavour of freshly laid eggs is equivalent to the taste of home grown vegetables. Keeping hens is enjoyable and popular with children. Hens' manure is ideal mixed into the compost heap, although it is too highly concentrated to be used directly on the land. You may need permission to keep livestock, so check with your local city ordinances regarding Bye-Laws.

Hens must have a suitable place to sleep and lay their eggs. A hen house for six chickens should be about 6 by 4 feet (180 by 120 cm). Construct it so that it faces south with plenty of window on that side to let in maximum sunlight which will encourage the hens to lay. Construct the nest box about 1 foot (30 cm) off the ground for purposes of hygiene. The floor should be of wood and covered in 6 inches (15 cm) of litter, which, after being used, can be added to the compost heap. This litter can be straw, sawdust, dry leaves, peat or bracken.

It is best not to let your hens out of their house too early in the morning as they may feel apt to lay eggs in places other than the nest box. You can let your hens roam in the garden; they are great for getting rid of unwanted pests. This is presuming you are not using chemical pesticides, which would poison the chickens. In the Summer, if they are allowed to forage in the garden, you need only feed them with grain. This you can buy by the sackload at farm feed outlets. Beware of buying feed containing chemicals. In the Winter, you will have to increase the variety of the food.

When I kept chickens I had a large saucepan in which I would cook a mash of potato peelings, stale bread and bran and allow to cool before serving. I always felt they would need a hearty breakfast! They also require fresh vegetables, which you can find in the garden, or ask your local vegetable shop for scraps. Hens also appreciate the addition of sunflower, alfalfa or lupin seeds which are all easy to grow yourself.

You need to clean the hen house once a week and fumigate it occasionally by burning dry herbs or juniper berries in a metal container, perforated to let the smell pervade. This will ensure there are no bugs to make the chickens ill. Kept clean, well fed, and given fresh water daily, they don't get sick.

MARCH

During March in Great Britain we have Mothering Sunday. In America it is celebrated in May and in both countries this provides the florists with one of their best days trading of the year. Originally this was a day on which young people in service were given a holiday to go home to visit their families. Time off was a rare occurrence in the old days and many children had to travel quite a distance to their homes. A Simnel Cake was often baked as a gift. Symbolically the cake was covered in marzipan and decorated with eleven marzipan balls to represent the Apostles, excluding Judas.

In March, the weather is notoriously unpredictable – the food markets are, too, with spring vegetables still pretty scarce. Vegetables definitely in season this month are root vegetables, leeks, onions, spring cabbages, and cauliflowers. To make a change from the root and onion crops that have been predominant during the last couple of months, I have included a recipe using broccoli and one with mushrooms (Macaroni with Broccoli and Blue Cheese Sauce, page 43; and Pasta Noodles with Mushrooms and Leeks, page 44). The basis for both these dishes is pasta, which is nourishing, filling and economical. It has an essential place in any vegetarian cook's store cupboard!

As for gardening, the days are getting longer, and the weather is warming up, so, if February was a dry month and the ground is not water-logged, it is possible to start digging. Digging ground that is too wet will make it too compact and sour. You can protect the ground during the Winter with sheets of cardboard covered with plastic. This helps to keep the soil warm. In March, you are still likely to get spells of frost.

If the weather has been kind, there are a number of crops you can plant later in the month: potatoes, broad beans, peas, salad crops, cabbage, and cauliflower.

HEALTHY BREAKFASTS

It is often said that the first meal of the day is the most important, but it is one that many people skimp on. Granola and yogurt is a nourishing, healthy breakfast that is easy to prepare and delicious to eat. If you have still got room – and time! – follow it up with home-made bread and marmalade (January) or a soft boiled egg and soldiers (opposite).

Granola

3 tbsp honey
2 tbsp vegetable oil
8 oz / 250 g / 3 cups rolled oatmeal
3 tbsp chopped nuts (I prefer hazelnuts)
2 tbsp desiccated coconut
3 tbsp sultanas or raisins
3 tbsp sunflower seeds
2 tbsp sesame seeds

Preheat oven to 300°F / 120°C / Mark 2. Stir the honey and oil in a pan over a low heat. Mix the remaining ingredients in a large bowl, then stir in the honey and oil. Spread the mixture onto baking sheets and bake for 30 minutes. Allow to cool thoroughly and then store in an airtight container. You can vary the ingredients as you like, keeping the amount constant. If you increase the dry ingredients, increase the oil and honey, too.

Yogurt

1 pint / 600 ml / 2⅔ cups cows milk
2 tbsp skimmed milk powder (this makes a
   good creamy yogurt)
1 tbsp live yogurt

This is simple to make provided that all your utensils are really clean. The cost of making it is very little compared to the cost of commercially produced yogurt. One of the easiest ways of making yogurt is to use a thermos flask. You can also buy special yogurt making machines.

Heat the milk to boiling point, remove from the heat and stir in the dried milk, if using. Allow the milk to cool to blood temperature – this means you can hold your finger in it at a comfortable heat. Stir in the live yogurt, mix thoroughly, and then pour into your sterile pot. If the container is not scrupulously clean, the yogurt will not set. Leave to set overnight in a warm place. Remember to reserve a little from each batch to start the next.

When you serve the yogurt you can eat it plain or sweeten it with honey, adding granola, fresh fruit, nuts or anything that takes your fancy.

Yogurt is a very healthy food as it contains bacteria which help the formation of beneficial bacteria in the intestines, aiding digestion. It contains large amounts of B vitamins and is high in protein and calcium. It is excellent if you have been on a course of antibiotics as it helps restore the balance of the intestinal flora.

Soft Boiled Egg

Place one egg in a pan of cold water and bring to the boil. When boiling, turn down the heat slightly so it is just on the boil. Cook for 1½ minutes. If the egg is really large, cook for an extra ½ minute. Place it in an egg cup, with a teaspoon on a side plate, and serve immediately as the egg still continues to cook in its shell. Nothing is worse than trying to dip your soldiers in an egg that is too hard!

Cream of Parsnip and Potato Soup

Roughly chop the vegetables. Cook the onion in a little oil to lightly brown it. Put the onion in a large pan with the stock, parsnips and potatoes. Cook for 15 minutes until soft. Cool and liquidize. Add the seasoning and return to the pan with the milk. Heat through gently for 10 minutes. Serve with parsley and croutons sprinkled on the top.

Croutons
Dice several slices of slightly stale bread, then fry them in shallow oil and butter. Turn them in order to brown them evenly. Remove and drain on kitchen paper. Store them in the freezer; alternatively they will keep for quite a while in an airtight container.

1 lb / 500 g / 3 cups parsnips
2 medium potatoes
1 large onion, finely chopped
1 pint / 600 ml / 2½ cups vegetable stock
salt and pepper
¼ tsp ground nutmeg
1 pint / 600 ml / 2½ cups milk
1 tbsp chopped parsley

Garlic Bread

This is delicious served with soup or any other vegetable type meals, and one occasion when butter definitely gives a superior flavour.

Crush the garlic and cream it with the salt, butter and milk. Add the parsley.

Cut the French stick in diagonal slices, being careful not to cut through completely. Spread the slices with the garlic and butter mixture, wrap the loaf in foil and bake for about 15 minutes at 400°F / 200°C / Mark 6. Serve immediately.

1 clove garlic
2 oz / 50 g / ¼ cup butter
1 tsp milk
1 tbsp chopped parsley
1 French stick

Hotch Potch Soup

1 large onion, finely sliced
1 clove garlic, crushed
2 medium parsnips
3 small leeks
½ shredded cabbage
2 sticks celery
4 carrots
salt and pepper
bouquet garni
3 pints / 1¾ litres / 7½ cups good vegetable
    stock
15oz / 400 g / 2 cups canned tomatoes
1 oz / 25 g / 1 cup cooked haricot beans or
    handful pasta shapes
chopped fresh parsley to garnish

This is a minestrone-type soup, and a good way of using up odd vegetables.

Scrub and dice all the vegetables. Heat a little oil in a large pan and fry the onion and garlic. Add the vegetables. Season with salt and pepper. Add the bouquet garni, stock and tomatoes. Bring to the boil and simmer for 30 minutes. Add the beans or pasta shapes a couple of minutes before the end of the cooking time. Remove the bouquet garni. Sprinkle the soup with the parsley and serve.

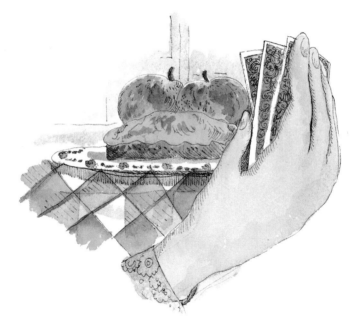

Welsh Rarebit

1½ oz / 30 g / 3 tablespoons butter
3 tbsp brown ale
salt
pepper
½ tsp English mustard
6 oz / 175 g / 1½ cups finely grated Cheddar
    cheese
pinch cayenne pepper
6 slices hot buttered toast

This is a recipe I remember well from my childhood days, especially from visiting my grandmother in Kent. She would very often prepare this as a supper dish when the family were sitting around playing cards.

Melt all the ingredients for the topping in a saucepan over a low heat. Stir continuously so the cheese does not stick. When melted, spread on the toast and place under the grill until golden brown.

Macaroni with Broccoli and Blue Cheese Sauce

Melt the margarine, add the flour, mustard powder, salt and pepper and cook for two minutes, stirring occasionally. Gradually stir in the milk, using a balloon whisk, as this prevents lumps forming. Stir briskly until smooth. Remove from the heat. Stir in the yogurt and blue Stilton cheese. Reserve a couple of spoonfuls of sauce for the top, and mix the remainder into the macaroni, gently folding in the broccoli. Grease an ovenproof dish, fill with the mixture, spread the remaining sauce on the top and bake for 20 minutes at 350°F / 180°C / Gas Mark 4.

8 oz / 250 g / 2 cups wholewheat macaroni, boiled for 10–12 minutes until just cooked
8 oz / 250 g / 2 cups broccoli, cooked for 3 minutes in boiling salted water
1 oz / 25 g / 2 tablespoons margarine
1 oz / 25 g / ¼ cup plain wholewheat flour
½ tsp dried mustard powder
salt and pepper to taste
¼ pint / 150 ml / ⅔ cup milk
5 oz / 125 g / ½ cup natural yogurt
6 oz / 175 g / 1½ cups Stilton cheese or other blue cheese

Tossed Cauliflower and Tofu

Use a wok if you have one. Melt the butter and cook the ginger, onion, and cauliflower for 2 or 3 minutes until the onion is golden brown. Pull up to one side of the wok. Put the arrowroot in the wok with the sugar and shoyu. Stir around until smooth. Draw the vegetables back in and cook for another 5 minutes. Add the tofu to the mixture. When it is heated through, sprinkle in the almonds, stir and serve.

2 tbsp butter
½ tsp grated fresh ginger root
1 small onion, chopped
1 small cauliflower, broken into florets
1 tsp arrowroot
1 tsp Demerara sugar
3 tbsp shoyu
5 oz / 125 g / 1 cup plain tofu (cut into small cubes about the size of the cauliflower pieces)
2 oz / 50 g / ½ cup flaked almonds

Pasta Noodles with Mushrooms and Leeks

8 oz / 250 g / 2 cups pasta noodles or ribbons, cooked for 10 minutes until just tender

1 large leek, washed and shredded

1 medium onion, finely chopped

4 oz / 125 g / 2 cups mushrooms, thinly sliced

1 oz / 25 g / 2 tablespoons margarine

1 oz / 25 g / ¼ cup plain wholewheat flour

½ tsp vegetable extract

salt and pepper to taste

¼ pint / 150 ml / ⅔ cup milk

1 tbsp fresh chopped parsley

1 tbsp grated Parmesan cheese

Fry the leek and onion gently in some oil until slightly softened. Add the mushrooms and cook until they soften. In a saucepan, melt the margarine, adding the flour and vegetable extract, salt and pepper. Cook for 2 minutes, stirring to mix. Slowly add the milk, stirring thoroughly. Stir in the fried vegetables and parsley. Tip the pasta into a buttered serving dish. Pour the sauce over the top, then sprinkle with the cheese. Put under a hot grill to melt the cheese and serve.

Russian Pie

1 onion, finely chopped

3 sticks celery, finely chopped

12 oz / 375 g / 6 cups finely chopped mushrooms

1 tsp vegetable extract

1 tbsp flour

3 hard-boiled eggs, finely chopped

salt and pepper

1 tbsp chopped parsley

1½ lb / 750 g / 5 cups mashed potato

few drops Tabasco

Sauce

½ pint / 300 ml / 1⅓ cups milk

slice raw onion

1 bayleaf

pinch of mace

5 peppercorns

3 tbsp butter

3 tbsp flour

First, make the sauce. Put the milk, onion and spices in a pan over a gentle heat and bring just to the boil. Rescue the pan from the heat, leave the milk to infuse for a few minutes, then strain.

In another pan, melt the butter and mix in the flour. Cook for two minutes. Mix in the strained milk, stirring continuously, until thickened.

For the pie, fry the onion and celery in a little oil until soft, add the mushrooms and cook until softened. Stir in the vegetable extract, flour, chopped eggs and seasoning. Stir in the sauce and parsley. Pour into a baking dish, and top with the mashed potato. Bake for 20 minutes until golden brown at 375°F / 190°C / Mark 5.

Raw Sugar Almond Paste/Marzipan

This will make about 2 lb / 1 kg of marzipan.

Sift the icing sugar into a bowl, and mix in the Muscovado sugar and almonds. Add the almond essence, and enough egg and lemon juice to form a stiff dough. Knead lightly. Place in a plastic bag to keep it pliable.

8 oz / 225 g / 1⅓ cups light Muscovado sugar, put through a blender to turn it into icing sugar
8 oz / 225 g / 1⅓ cups light Muscovado sugar
1 lb / 450 g / 4 cups ground almonds
1 tsp almond essence
2 medium eggs, lightly beaten
lemon juice

Simnel Cake

Cream the butter and sugar together until light, fluffy and pale in colour. Beat in the eggs one at a time. Add a little of the flour to prevent the eggs curdling. Sift in the remaining flour, baking powder and spices. Fold in the dried fruit, rind and juices. Pour half the mixture into a greased, lined 8 inch (20 cm) cake tin.

Roll out the marzipan into an 8 inch circle and place on top of the mixture in the tin. Pour the remaining mixture on top. In a preheated 325°F / 170°C / Mark 3 oven, bake for 2–2½ hours, or until a skewer inserted into the cake comes away clean. Allow the cake to cool for a few minutes in the tin and then turn onto a wire rack.

When the cake is completely cool, paint the top with the jam. Roll out the marzipan into an 8 inch circle and eleven small balls. Crimp the edges of the circle and place on the cake. Dab a little jam underneath the balls and arrange them on the cake. Put the cake under a fairly hot grill for a few seconds to brown it slightly. Finish by tying a nice ribbon around it.

6 oz / 175 g / ¾ cup unsalted butter or margarine (the cake will keep better if butter is used)
6 oz / 175 g / 1 cup light Muscovado sugar
3 medium eggs
8 oz / 220 g / 2 cups plain wholewheat flour
1 tsp baking powder
1 tsp ground cloves
1 tsp ground cinnamon
1 tsp ground nutmeg
6 oz / 175 g / 1 cup sultanas
4 oz / 100 g / ⅔ cup raisins
grated rind and juice of 1 orange and 1 lemon
8 oz / 220 g / 1 block raw sugar marzipan

To decorate
3 tbsp apricot jam
13 oz / 350 g / 1½ blocks marzipan

Fudge Tart

Flan case
6 oz / 175 g / 1½ cups plain wholewheat
flour
2 oz / 50 g / ½ cup ground almonds
4 oz / 100 g / ½ cup vegetable margarine

Filling
5 oz / 125 g / ⅞ cup dark Muscovado sugar
2 tbsp butter
¼ tsp vanilla extract
pinch salt
1 beaten egg
3 oz / 75 g / ¾ cup chopped walnuts
3 oz / 75 g / ½ cup raisins

This is a rich, sticky dessert ideal for a special occasion.

For the flan case, mix the flour and almonds together, then rub in the margarine until the mixture looks like fine breadcrumbs. Add about 3–4 tbsp cold water and mix to make a soft dough. Roll the dough out on a floured board and use it to line a 9 inch (22 cm) flan tin. Prebake for 15 minutes at 400°F / 200°C / Mark 6. Allow to cool.

Reduce the heat to 325°F / 170°C / Mark 3. Beat the sugar, butter, vanilla and salt together until creamy. Add the egg and beat well, then stir in the nuts and raisins. Pour the filling into the flan case and bake for 25 minutes.

Shortbread

4 oz / 125 g / ⅔ cup light Muscovado sugar
8 oz / 250 g / 2 cups plain flour
4 oz / 125 g / 1 cup rice flour
8 oz / 250 g / 1 cup butter

Mix the sugar, flour and rice flour together. Rub in the butter. When the dough is holding together, press it into a lightly greased 8 inch (20 cm) sandwich tin. Prick the top with a fork and crimp around the edges to decorate. Bake for 45 minutes at 300°F / 150°C / Mark 2.

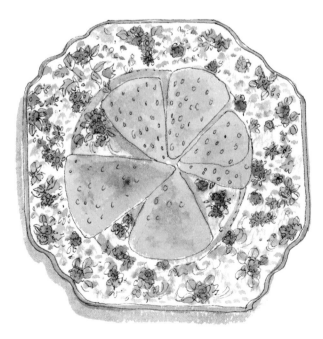

Pineapple Squares (sugar free)

Preheat the oven to 350°F / 180°C / Mark 4. Finely chop the pineapple. Separate the egg and whisk the white until frothy. Beat in the pineapple juice and pineapple. Stir in the other ingredients, including the egg yolk. Pour into greased and lined 7 inch (18 cm) square baking tin. Bake for 40–45 minutes until firm. Cut into squares and allow to cool in the tin. Store in an airtight container.

15 oz / 450 g / 2 cups canned pineapple in natural juice
1 large beaten egg
6 oz / 175 g / 2 cups desiccated coconut
3 oz / 75 g / ¾ cup wholewheat flour
1 oz / 25 g / ¼ cup rice flour
pinch salt

Sesame Squares (sugar free)

Bring the sesame seeds, raisins and water to the boil in a saucepan. Add the vanilla extract and peanut butter. Cook for a further 2 minutes until a sticky paste is formed. Add the chopped peanuts to the mixture. Press into a well-greased 7 inch (18 cm) square shallow tin. Chill in the refrigerator for an hour. Cut into squares and store in an airtight container.

6 oz / 175 g / 1½ cups sesame seeds
8 oz / 200 g / ¾ cup chopped raisins
¼ pint / 140 ml / ⅔ cup water
¼ tsp vanilla extract
6 oz / 175 g / ¾ cup smooth peanut butter (page 62)
3 oz / 75 g / ¾ cup finely chopped peanuts

PEST CONTROL AND COMPANION PLANTING

Now just a few lines on the natural way to control pests and a subject which goes hand in hand with it – companion planting.

It is amazing just how quickly slugs can devour your new plants. Try using grapefruit skins cut side down – the slugs will crawl under them and then you can remove and dispose of them. Or place a tile 1½ inches (4 cm) above soaked earth and put lettuce leaves or oranges under the tile. After about two weeks lift the tile and remove the slugs. Or place a saucer of beer out, and the slugs will crawl in and drown. The amount of slugs you can collect in one year is colossal. If you can befriend a hedgehog, that will do a lot of the work for you, as slugs are one of their favourite foods. Centipedes, too, eat troublesome bugs. It is better not to treat with chemicals as the life cycle of many creatures can be affected.

Wormwood is a good border plant to grow as it keeps aphids away.

There are some plants that like to be grown near each other; others have a detrimental effect. Broccoli grows well with aromatic plants such as dill, celery, peppermint, rosemary and sage. The same goes for the rest of the cabbage family. Potatoes like rosemary but dislike tomatoes, strawberries, and runner beans. Potatoes are heavy feeders so need a lot of compost.

Asparagus grows well with parsley and basil. Basil improves growth and flavour of tomatoes, it also cooks with tomatoes very well. Beans grow well with carrots, cauliflower, beetroot, and sweetcorn. Onions inhibit the growth of beans. Borage around strawberry beds is helpful.

Carrots grow with onions, leeks, and flavourful herbs. For sweet carrots use lime, potash, and a lot of humus.

Work with nature in the garden, and you will be rewarded both your produce and also by the wildlife that will be attracted. If the weather has been kind, some of the things that can be planted later this month are potatoes, broad beans, peas, salad crops, cabbage and cauliflower.

APRIL

April showers, April Fools and Easter all appear this month. Hot Cross Buns are traditionally eaten on Good Friday and, up until a few years ago, were only available on Good Friday. Now they seem to appear in the shops almost as soon as the Christmas decorations are cleared away. The best kind, of course, are home made. Bake them the day before to make it easier for yourself, or make a batch in advance and freeze them (recipe on page 55).

Easter wouldn't be Easter without an abundance of eggs. The custom of exchanging decorated eggs at this time of the year is a very ancient one. Steer the children away from too many of the chocolate variety by getting them to decorate hens' eggs. Pierce holes in each end and blow out the contents. (You can use that to cook with.) Paint the surface with egg white – this will make it smooth for painting. The children can run riot here; any kind of colouring materials can be used to make faces and patterns; glue on scraps of wool for hair. Not acrylic or oil paints though; we don't want to poison the children.

Root crops have dwindled away a bit, but broccoli, spinach and cauliflower are good, and I've made the most of them with this month's recipes. April is the time for rhubarb crops – exploit yours by making jam (page 57), Rhubarb and Raspberry Crumble (page 56), and a delicious, tangy sauce to serve with lentil cutlets (page 57).

This is the ideal month to try and get a herb garden started. Buy the ones which you use frequently and try to plant them fairly close to the house. It will be more of an incentive to use them in cooking if they are readily available. If you have the time and energy, you can raise herbs from seed.

It is time to start planting the garden. The earth is warming up, and the sooner it gets planted, the sooner there will be less room for weeds.

Spinach Soup

1 oz / 25 g / 2 tbsp margarine
1 large onion, finely chopped
2 tbsp flour
2 tbsp lemon juice
½ tsp nutmeg
½ tsp paprika
2 pints / 1¼ litres / 5 cups vegetable stock
1½ lb / 750 g / 6 cups shredded spinach
salt and pepper to taste
¼ pint / 150 ml / 1 cup creamy milk

Melt the margarine and gently fry the onion until it is golden brown. Stir in the flour and cook for 2 minutes. Add the lemon juice, spices and vegetable stock. Add the spinach, cover and simmer for half an hour until tender. Allow to cool, then liquidize. Return to the pan. Season, add the milk, gently reheat and serve.

Vegetable Pâté

1 lb / 500 g / 4 cups whole spinach leaves
2 oz / 50 g / ¼ cup margarine
1 medium onion, finely chopped
2 large carrots
2 medium potatoes, grated
4 oz / 125 g / 1 cup finely chopped celery
2 oz / 50 g / ½ cup wholemeal flour
1 tsp vegetable extract
1 tsp dried thyme
salt and pepper to taste
2 eggs
2 oz / 50 g / ½ cup wheatgerm

Preheat the oven to 350°F / 180°C / Mark 4. Grease a 2 lb / 1 kg loaf tin. Line the tin with the washed spinach. Overlap the leaves on the inside and leave enough overhang to cover the top when completed. There will be some spinach remaining; cook this gently in a covered pan in a little milk. In another pan melt the margarine and cook the onion until transparent, add the carrots, potato and celery and cook for 1 minute. Stir in the flour and cook for a further minute.

Strain the spinach and add it to the vegetables, then make the spinach liquor up to ¼ pint / 150 ml / ⅔ cup with water. Pour this into the pan of vegetables and add the vegetable extract, thyme, salt and pepper.

Away from the heat, beat in the eggs and wheatgerm. Press the pâté into the loaf tin and fold the spinach over the top. Cover with foil and place the tin in a pan of boiling water to prevent the eggs from curdling. Bake the pâté for 1 hour. Allow the pâté to cool before turning it out onto a serving dish. Although this slices well when cold, it tastes good hot.

Cheese Pâté

Bring the milk to boiling point. Add the vegetables and bouquet garni and simmer for 15 minutes until the vegetables are very soft. Strain the milk into a bowl. Melt the margarine in a pan, add the flour and cook for 2 minutes. Then stir in the strained milk, to make a smooth sauce. When cool, stir in the mayonnaise, lemon juice, garlic, olives and cayenne pepper. Season with salt and pepper. Beat in the cheese and spoon into a pâté dish. Chill until firm and serve.

1¼ pints / 750 ml / 3⅓ cups milk
1 large finely chopped onion
1 large carrot, finely grated
2 sticks celery, finely chopped
1 bouquet garni
3 oz / 40 g / ⅓ cup margarine
3 oz / 40 g / ¾ cup flour
3 tbsp mayonnaise
2 tsp lemon juice
3 cloves garlic, crushed
2 oz / 50 g / ⅓ cup green olives, chopped
pinch cayenne pepper
salt and pepper
12 oz / 375 g / 3 cups Stilton cheese or blue cheese rubbed once through a sieve

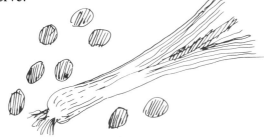

Leeks à la Grèque

This is an easy starter – just serve it with hot crusty bread.

Heat the oil in a pan. Add the leeks and garlic and fry for 5 minutes. Add the water, including the bouquet garni, wine and seasoning. Bring to the boil then simmer gently for 40 minutes with the lid on. Remove the lid and remove the bouquet garni. Continue to simmer for 5 minutes. Allow to cool and then serve garnished with the parsley.

4 tbsp Greek Olive oil
1 lb / 500 g / 4 cups leeks, trimmed, washed and sliced into 3 inch (8 cm) pieces
2 cloves garlic, crushed
⅛ pint / 75 ml / ¼ cup each of water and white wine
salt, pepper, pinch ground mace
1 bouquet garni
chopped parsley to garnish

Stuffed Baked Onions

Boil the onions in their skins for 10–15 minutes, until slightly softened. Remove the skins, and carefully remove the centres of the onions and finely chop them. Heat the butter or margarine in a pan. Fry the chopped onion in the butter for a couple of minutes. Add the flour and cook another 2 minutes. Stir in the milk and cheese, reserving a little cheese for the topping. When the mixture is thick, stir in ⅔ of the breadcrumbs and the pine kernels. Season with basil, salt and pepper. Use this mixture to stuff into the centres of the onions.

Place the onions in an ovenproof dish and sprinkle with the remaining Parmesan cheese and breadcrumbs. Press down slightly. Mix 2 tbsp oil and 2 tbsps water together and pour into the dish. Bake at 375°F / 190°C / Mark 5 for 30 minutes, basting occasionally.

6 large Spanish onions
2 tbsp butter or margarine
1 oz / 25 g / ¼ cup flour
¼ pint / 150 ml / ⅔ cup milk
2 oz / 50 g / ½ cup Parmesan cheese
6 oz / 150 g / 3 cups wholemeal breadcrumbs
4 oz / 125 g / 1 cup pine kernels
1 tsp basil
salt and pepper

Spinach Roulade

¾ pint / ½ litre / 2 cups milk
1 lb / 500 g / 16 cups washed spinach
3 oz / 40 g / ⅓ cup butter
3 oz / 40 g / ¾ cup flour
4 eggs, separated
salt, pepper and ground nutmeg to season

Filling
3 hard-boiled eggs
1 tbsp grated Parmesan cheese
salt and pepper

Filling
6 oz / 150 g / 1 cup butterbeans (soaked overnight)
1 lb / 500 g / 2 spears broccoli
1 medium onion, finely chopped
1 tsp vegetable extract
2 oz / 50 g / ¼ cup margarine
2 oz / 50 g / ½ cup flour
¾ pint / ½ litre / 2 cups milk
4 tbsp chopped fresh parsley
salt and pepper to taste

Pancakes
8 oz / 250 g / 2 cups wholemeal flour
1 egg
½ pint / ¼ litre / 1¼ cups milk
pinch salt
1 tbsp oil

Use a little of the milk to cook the spinach for 3 minutes. Strain and squeeze out the excess liquid; reserve for later. Melt the butter in a saucepan. Add the flour and cook for 2 minutes. Gradually stir in the rest of the milk and the reserved spinach liquid. Stir thoroughly to make a smooth sauce.

Put half of the sauce in a bowl with the spinach and egg yolks. Reserve the remainder for filling. Season the spinach mixture with salt, pepper and a pinch of ground nutmeg. Whisk the egg whites until they are really stiff, then carefully fold them into the spinach mixture with a metal spoon. Pour this into a greased and lined 12 by 6 inch (30 by 15 cm) Swiss roll tin and bake at 375°F / 190°C / Mark 5 for 20–25 minutes until set and slightly brown. Allow to cool and remove the wax paper.

For the filling, stir the chopped egg into the remaining sauce along with the cheese and salt and pepper. Spread the filling over the roll and carefully roll it up quite tightly. Wrap it in wax paper and allow to set in the refrigerator. Unwrap the roll when you are ready to serve it. It will cut into nice slices.

Butterbean and Broccoli Pancakes

Drain the butterbeans and cover them with fresh water. Bring them to the boil, reduce the heat and simmer for 1–1½ hours, until tender. Cook the broccoli in boiling salted water for 5 minutes and then drain. Fry the onion in a little oil until it just starts to brown. When soft, stir in the vegetable extract and margarine. Allow to melt, then stir in the flour and cook for 2 minutes. Gradually stir in the milk, mixing thoroughly to prevent lumping. Season with the parsley, salt and pepper. Mix the broccoli and butterbeans in with the sauce (first reserving a little sauce to top the finished dish).

Sift the flour for the pancakes and drop the egg into it. Beat in the milk a little at a time, add the salt and oil and beat well. Heat a pan and pour in a little oil. Drop a little of the batter into the pan so that the bottom is covered. Cook until brown then turn the pancake over and cook the other side. Stuff the pancake with the filling, fold in the ends, then roll it up. Continue in the same manner with the rest of the batter. Place the pancakes in a greased ovenproof dish and cover with the reserved sauce. For a little extra colour, you can sprinkle cheese over the top. Bake for 15 minutes at 350°F / 180°C / Mark 4.

Hot Cross Buns

This recipe should make 12 buns, depending on the size you prefer.

For the buns, stir the yeast with 1 tsp sugar and a little of the milk – leave to get frothy. Meanwhile, sift the flour, salt, spices and remaining sugar into a mixing bowl. Stir in the fruit. Mix the melted margarine in with the rest of the milk. Make a well in the centre of the flour and pour in the yeast and milk mixture and the milk and margarine. Mix until you have a smooth, elastic dough. Cover the bowl and leave until the dough has doubled in size. Place the dough on a work top divide into 12 and reknead. Put the buns on a greased baking tray, cover and leave to rise again.

Meanwhile, mix together the ingredients for the crosses. Use a piping bag with a small nozzle to pipe crosses onto the buns. (Or use a small plastic bag with a tiny piece cut off the corner and force the paste out through this.) Put the buns in a preheated 425°F / 220°C / Mark 7 oven for 15 minutes.

Boil the glaze ingredients to make a syrup and brush with this glaze as soon as the buns are out of the oven. Cool on a wire rack and resist all temptation to eat immediately.

1 oz / 30 g / 1 cake compressed fresh yeast or ½ oz tbsp dried yeast

2 oz / 60 g / ⅓ cup Muscovado sugar

½ pint / 300 ml / 1⅓ cup hand-hot milk

1 lb / 500 g / 4 cups wholemeal flour or 1 lb / 500 g / 4 cups strong white flour (or a mixture of the two)

½ tsp salt

½ tsp each ground cinnamon, nutmeg and cloves

½ tsp mixed spice

6 oz / 180 g / 1 cup cake fruit – 4 oz / 125 g / ⅔ cup currants and 2 oz / 60 g / ⅓ cup mixed cut peel is usual

2 oz / 60 g / ¼ cup melted margarine

Paste Crosses

1½ oz / 40 g / ⅓ cup strong white flour (wholemeal is trickier to handle as it goes stringy)

1 tbsp vegetable oil

3 tbsp water

Glaze

¼ pint / 15 cl / ⅔ cup water

2 oz / 50 g / ⅓ cup Demerara sugar

Easter Biscuits

4 oz / 125 g / ½ cup butter or margarine
3 oz / 95 g / ½ cup light Muscovado sugar
1 egg, separated
8 oz / 250 g / 2 cups plain flour
pinch salt
½ tsp ground cassia (1 tsp cinnamon if
   cassia unobtainable)
1 tsp ground mixed spice
2 oz / 50 g / ¼ cup currants
1–2 tbsp milk

Cream the butter and sugar until they are fluffy. Reserving 1 tbsp egg white, beat the remaining egg yolk and white into the butter. Stir in the flour, salt and spices. Fold in the currants and add the milk.

Knead the dough lightly on a floured work top. Roll out ⅛ inch (5mm) thick. This is easier if you let the dough rest for half an hour first. Cut out the biscuits using a 3 inch (8 cm) cutter. Place on lightly greased trays. Brush with the egg white. Sprinkle with Demerara sugar. Bake at 400°F / 200°C / Mark 6 for 12 minutes until lightly golden. Cool on a wire rack.

Pastry
8 oz / 250 g / 2 cups plain wholemeal flour
4 oz / 125 g / ½ cup margarine

Filling
2 tbsp flour
4 oz / 125 g / 1 cup ground almonds
4 oz / 125 g / ½ cup unsalted butter
4 oz / 125 g / ⅔ cup light Muscovado sugar
2 eggs, beaten
rind of 2 lemons

Topping
2 lemons, thinly sliced, seeds removed
1 pint / 60 cl / 2½ cups water
14 oz / 425 g / 2⅓ cups Demerara sugar

Lemon Tart

Rub the fat into the flour. Add the cold water to make a dough. Roll out pastry and line a 10 inch (24 cm) pie dish. Bake blind with wax paper and baking beans for 10 minutes at 425°F / 220°C / Mark 7.

For the filling, mix the flour and almonds together. Beat butter and sugar together until fluffy. Add the egg and lemon rind. Add the flour mixture and spread in the pastry case. Bake for 25 minutes at 375°F / 190°C / Mark 5, until firm and golden.

For the topping, place the lemon slices and water in a saucepan and simmer gently for ½ hour. Remove the lemon slices and drain. Add the sugar to the water and bring to the boil. Replace the lemon slices and cook gently for 10 minutes. Remove the lemon slices and arrange on the top of the tart. Boil the liquid until thick, then pour over the tart and chill. Serve.

Topping
4 oz / 125 g / ½ cup melted margarine
4 oz / 125 g / 1½ cups rolled oats
4 oz / 125 g / ⅔ cup Demerara sugar
2 oz / 60 g / ½ cup finely chopped hazelnuts
2 oz / 60 g / ½ cup wholemeal flour
1 tsp ground cinnamon

Filling
1 lb / 500 g / 4 cups trimmed rhubarb
8 oz / 250 g / 2 cups raspberries

Rhubarb and Raspberry Crumble

Rub the ingredients for the topping together. Simmer the rhubarb in a little water for 5 minutes. Mix the raspberries and rhubarb together in an ovenproof dish. Sprinkle the topping over. Bake at 375°F / 190°C / Mark 5 for 40 minutes until golden brown. Serve hot or cold.

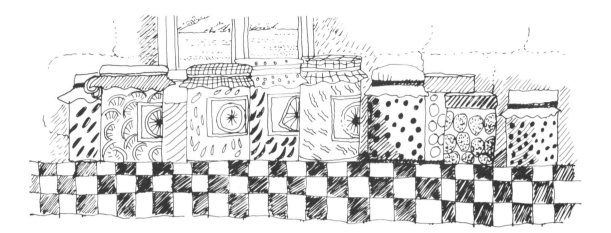

Lemon (or Orange) Curd

Grate the lemon or orange rind and squeeze the juice. Put the butter in a pan with the sugar and rind and juice. Cook gently until the sugar has dissolved. Remove from the heat and add the eggs. Then cook slowly, stirring all the time, until the mixture thickens. Cook for a further 1–2 minutes but do not boil. The consistency should be like thick custard. It thickens further while it is cooling. Bottle the lemon curd (page 16).

4 oz / 125 g / ½ cup butter
10 oz / 300 g / 1⅔ cups Demerara sugar
8 oz / 250 g / 2 medium lemons or oranges
2 eggs, well beaten

Rhubarb and Ginger Jam

Cut the rhubarb into pieces, place in a bowl and sprinkle it with the sugar and lemon juice. Next day, bruise the ginger with a hammer. Tie it in a piece of muslin, and place in a pan with the rhubarb and sugar. Bring to the boil and boil rapidly for 15 minutes. Remove the ginger, add the crystallized ginger and boil for a further 5 minutes until the jam is clear and setting point is reached. Pot the jam (page 16).

2½ lb / 1 kg / 10 cups rhubarb
2½ lb / 1 kg / 6⅔ cups Demerara sugar
5 tbsp lemon juice
3 x 1 inch (2.5 cm) pieces bruised root ginger
4 oz / 125 g / ⅔ cup crystallized ginger, finely chopped

Rhubarb Sauce

This is delicious with lentil or bean cutlets.
   Heat the oil and fry the onion for 10 minutes without browning. Cut rhubarb into 3 inch (8 cm) pieces. Add the rhubarb to the onions with the sugar, vinegar and salt and pepper. Simmer for 20 minutes with the lid on the pan, until the rhubarb is soft. Remove the lid and continue to simmer until thick. This sauce keeps in the refrigerator for up to three days.

½ tbsp vegetable oil
1 large onion, finely chopped
12 oz / 375 g / 3 cups trimmed, washed rhubarb
4 oz / 125 g / ⅔ cup Demerara sugar
2 tbsp red wine vinegar
salt and pepper

MAY

There are a couple of Bank Holidays in May – May Day and Whitsun – so this will give you a little extra time for the garden, with any luck!

During May, with the weather warming, many children will be thinking of taking a packed lunch to school. I have included a few ideas for this. Try and steer your children away from ready prepared foods bought at the supermarket. Substitute something prepared at home that will provide the vitamins and fibre needed to keep young growing bodies in good health now and lay the foundations for good health later on: what they eat now will determine their health in ten years time.

We all know that children like the kind of food that is not necessarily good for them. Usually it is the type of thing that is likely to worsen skin conditions such as acne and eczema, and aggravate hyperactivity. A diet high in fibre is filling and can actually help to reduce weight.

You will probably find that a child on a well-balanced diet is fairly resistant to colds and 'flu and all manner of other bugs that seem to fly around the playground. An adequate supply of Vitamin C and A are especially important. A shortage of B vitamins can cause effects on mood, such as loss of memory and depression. Research shows that there may be links between bad diet and hyperactivity and juvenile delinquency, so try and guard against them with an adequate diet.

This month you should start getting some produce from the garden. Broad beans, beetroot, gooseberries and carrots should all be ready towards the end of the month. Avocados are good in the vegetable shops; the crinkly dark skinned ones (usually from Israel) have a lovely flavour. There are small pineapples which are plentiful and cheap. Now is the time to sow outdoor cucumbers, runner beans, marrows and tomatoes, and plant celeriac, leeks and celery.

PACKED LUNCHES

The packed lunch can be just as nourishing as a cooked lunch, and as the weather gets warmer, it's an instant picnic! It will contain plenty of protein if you use egg, cheese or nut butter as a base for a wholemeal bread sandwich. Add a piece of fresh fruit and a slice of wholemeal cake or biscuit. In cold weather, a flask of homemade soup is a lovely warm thing to give. You can buy a special flask which is unbreakable and keeps soup hot for a few hours.

Peanut Butter

Peanut butter is a good staple for sandwiches. Try and buy the type that has no sugar added. It is possible to make your own. There are special machines on the market for it but I find my blender adequate – or you could use a food processor. Roasting ordinary shelled peanuts in a moderate oven for a few minutes enhances the flavour. Put the nuts in your blender with a little oil and salt and run until smooth or crunchy, depending on taste. You may need to stop and give it a stir, as it does tend to clog up. 1 lb / 500g / 2 cups peanuts will make a couple of large jars of butter. If it feels stiff just add a little more vegetable oil. Keep the jars in the refrigerator as this stops it going rancid. There are no preservatives in it, so it won't keep indefinitely.

Sandwich Ideas

Here are just a few ideas, some of the fillings favoured by my children and their friends. They seem to hold sampling sessions at lunch times. Double decker sandwiches are really popular, provided the bread is thinly sliced.

Peanut butter and honey.
Peanut butter and banana.
Peanut butter and alfalfa sprouts.
Curd cheese and pineapple.
Curd cheese and cucumber.
Curd cheese and chopped onion.
Banana and chopped dates.
Cheese and grated carrot.
Cheese, yeast extract, lettuce, tomato and mayonnaise.
Chopped egg.
Chopped egg and cress.

Avocado Mousse

Cut each avocado in half, remove the stones and scoop out all the flesh into a bowl using a tablespoon, taking care not to break the shell. Add the other ingredients to the bowl and mix until light and fluffy. Spoon back into the shells and chill until needed. Cover with plastic film if not using immediately, or leave the mixture in the bowl and put in an avocado stone with it to prevent discoloration. Then fill the shells just before serving.

3 very ripe avocados
salt and pepper
3 tsp lemon juice
¼ tsp Tabasco sauce
1 tsp shoyu
3 tbsp soft low-fat cream cheese

Celery Soup

Fry the onion gently in the butter or margarine until transparent. Add the flour and cook for two minutes. Add the water and extract gradually, stirring until absorbed and thickened. Stir in the potatoes and celery, and cook for 15 minutes. Stir continually to prevent sticking. Stir in the milk, parsley, paprika and seasoning. Put ¾ of the soup through a blender then return to the pan with the other vegetables and serve.

½ onion, finely chopped
1 oz / 25 g / 2 tbsp butter or margarine
1 oz / 25 k / 1 cup flour
¼ pint / 150 ml / ⅓ cup water and 1 tsp
   vegetable extract
2 medium potatoes, scrubbed and diced
1 head celery, washed and diced
1½ pints / 1 litre / 3¾ cups milk
2 tbsp chopped fresh parsley
1 tsp paprika
⅛ tsp ground nutmeg
salt and pepper

Broad Beans in White Sauce

2 lb / 1 kg / 6 cups broad beans in pods
1 tsp finely chopped shallot or onion
5 tbsp white wine
3 tbsp white wine vinegar
1 tbsp thick strained yogurt
3 oz / 75 g / 1 cup unsalted butter
salt and pepper to taste

Take the beans from their pods. (You can use the pods for vegetable stock.) Simmer the beans gently for 6–7 minutes in a little water. Put the shallot, wine and vinegar in a saucepan, and simmer until the liquid has reduced by half. Add the yogurt, bring to the boil, then reduce the heat immediately. Stir in the butter, a little at a time, and keep stirring until smooth. Season with salt and pepper. Drain the beans and put them in a serving dish. Pour the sauce over the top. Serve immediately.

Tagliatelle with Avocado

1 lb / 500 g / 4 cups green tagliatelle
1 medium onion, finely chopped
5 fl oz / 150 ml / ⅔ cup yogurt or single cream
salt, pepper and a little nutmeg
4 firm tomatoes, chopped
2 avocados with the flesh cut into strips and soaked in 1 tbsp lemon juice
grated Parmesan cheese

Cook the tagliatelle. Fry the onion in a little oil until soft. When the pasta is cooked (about 12 minutes), put it into a bowl to keep warm. Stir in the onion, yogurt or cream and seasoning. Toss in the tomatoes. Arrange the avocado on the top. Sprinkle with Parmesan cheese and serve.

Celery and Mushroom Crumble

Mix together the ingredients for the crumble topping. Rub the margarine in.

For the filling, melt the margarine, and sauté the onion and celery for 5 minutes until soft. Add the mushrooms and tomatoes and cook for a further 2 minutes. Stir in the vegetable extract, flour, wine, milk and Tabasco. Cook for 10 minutes. Stir in the parsley and seasoning. Pour this mixture into a greased ovenproof dish. Sprinkle the crumble mixture over the top. Bake at 325°F / 170°C / Mark 3 for 40 minutes, or until golden brown.

Crumble Mixture
8 oz / 250 g / 2 cups plain wholemeal flour
2 oz / 60 g / ½ cup finely chopped nuts
4 oz / 125 g / ½ cup vegetable margarine
2 oz / 60 g / ½ cup sesame seeds
4 oz / 125 g / 1 cup grated Cheddar cheese

Celery Mixture
2 oz / 50 g / ¼ cup margarine
1 large onion, finely chopped
5 stalks celery, chopped
8 oz / 250 g / 4 cups sliced button
    mushrooms
6 tomatoes, chopped
1 tsp vegetable extract
2 oz / 50 g / ½ cup flour
¾ pint / 450 ml / 2 cups white wine
½ pint / 300 ml / 1¼ cups milk
dash Tabasco sauce
2 tbsp chopped parsley
salt and pepper

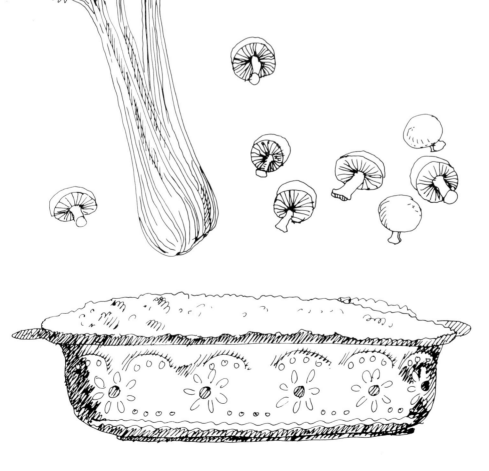

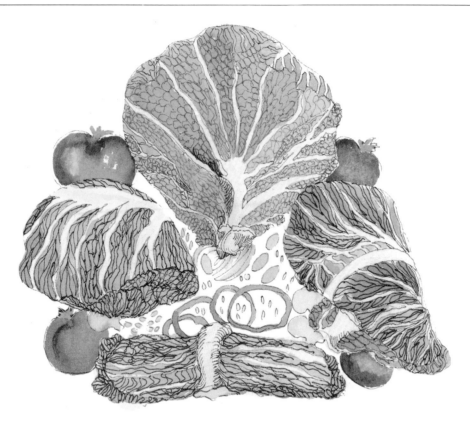

Stuffed Cabbage Parcels

1 large cabbage (Savoy is the easiest to use)

Filling
1 medium onion, finely chopped
4 green peppers, sliced
½ lb / 250 g / 4 cups thinly sliced
   mushrooms
8 oz / 250 g / 1 cup cooked brown rice
¼ pint / 150 ml / ⅔ cup vegetable stock
1 tsp ground coriander
pinch of mace
2 eggs
6 tsp roasted sunflower seeds

Sauce
1 oz / 25 g / 2 tablespoons margarine
1 oz / 25 g / ¼ cup flour
¼ pint / 150 ml / ⅔ cup vegetable stock
14 oz / 400 g / 2 cups canned tomatoes
juice of ½ lemon
salt and pepper

You will need two cabbage leaves per person. Remove the core from the cabbage and steam it whole for 5 minutes. Peel off 12 large leaves, or 18 if the cabbage is small. Preheat the oven to 350°F / 180°C / Mark 4.

For the filling, sauté the onion in a little oil. Stir, then add the green pepper and mushrooms. Sauté for 3 minutes. Stir in the cooked rice and sauté a few minutes longer. Add the stock and seasonings. Simmer over a low heat for 30 minutes until the vegetables are soft. Stir in the eggs and sunflower seeds.

For the sauce, melt the margarine, add the flour and cook for 2 minutes. Gradually add the stock and tomatoes. Stir and simmer for 30 minutes until thick. Stir in the lemon juice and seasoning a few minutes before the end of cooking time.

To assemble the parcels, place a spoonful of stuffing in the middle of each leaf. Fold the stem end over the stuffing, then fold the sides in and then the top over to the middle. Pour some sauce into the bottom of a greased ovenproof dish. Place the cabbage parcels side by side on top of that. Pour the rest of the sauce over the top and bake for 30 minutes. Baste with the sauce during cooking if the rolls are looking dry.

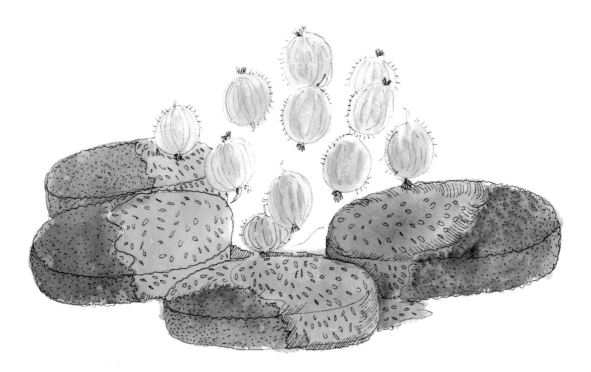

Lentil Burgers and Gooseberry Sauce

Wash the lentils. Pour the water into a large pan and add the lentils, then bring to the boil and simmer gently for about 1 hour, until mushy. Heat the margarine in a pan and sauté the onion, garlic and carrot for 5 minutes. Then add the green pepper and cook for a further 5 or 10 minutes. Tip the lentils into a bowl and mash them. Mix in the sautéed vegetables, tomato purée, herbs and spices. Divide into 12 burgers and brush each with egg and breadcrumbs. Fry in shallow oil until golden.

For the sauce, fry the onion in the margarine until light golden brown. Put the gooseberries in a pan with the water and add all the other ingredients. Cook until the fruit is tender, then strain through a sieve. Serve as an accompaniment to the lentil burgers.

8 oz / 250 g / 1¼ cups light green lentils
¾ pint / 450 ml / 2 cups water
2 oz / 50 g / ¼ cup margarine
1 medium onion, peeled and finely chopped
1 clove garlic, crushed
1 medium carrot, finely chopped
1 medium green pepper, finely chopped
2 tsp tomato pureé
½ tsp mixed herbs
¼ tsp ground mace
½ tsp cayenne pepper
egg and breadcrumbs to coat

Gooseberry Sauce

1 small onion or shallot, finely chopped
1 tbsp margarine
8 oz / 250 g / 2 cups gooseberries
2 tbsp water
1 tbsp chopped parsley
2 tbsp dry white wine
salt and pepper
2 tbsp Muscovado sugar
½ tsp dry mustard powder

Carob Florentines

3 oz / 75 g / ⅓ cup butter or margarine
4 tbsp milk
4 oz / 125 g / ⅔ cup light Muscovado sugar
1½ oz / 40 g / ⅓ cup plain wholemeal flour
2 oz / 50 g / ½ cup flaked almonds
2 oz / 50 g / 1 cup dried apricots (soaked overnight in a little water, drained and then chopped)

Topping
two 2 oz / 50 g carob bars
1 tsp butter

Melt the butter or margarine in a saucepan, then stir in the milk and sugar. Remove from the heat. Stir in all the other ingredients. Transfer the mixture to a bowl, and refrigerate for half an hour. Put small teaspoonfuls on a baking sheet 3 inches (7 cm) apart. Bake the florentines for 10–12 minutes at 375°F / 190°C / Mark 5. Allow to cool on a tray. Melt the carob bars and butter in a bowl over a pan of boiling water. Spread the carob on top of the florentines, then mark with a fork to decorate.

Malty Flapjack

3 oz / 75 g / ⅓ cup butter or margarine
3 oz / 75 g / ½ cup Demerara sugar
2 tbsp malt
6 oz / 150 g / 2 cups rolled oats

Melt the margarine, sugar and malt together in a saucepan. Mix in the oats and stir well to combine. Press lightly into a greased 7 by 9 inch (18 by 22 cm) Swiss roll tin. Bake at 350°F / 180°C / Mark 4 for 20–25 minutes, until light golden brown. They harden up during cooking, so cut them into fingers while still hot.

Coconut Macaroons

2 oz / 50 g / ⅔ cup desiccated coconut
1 oz / 25 g / ¼ cup ground rice
3 oz / 75 g / ½ cup light Muscovado sugar
1 egg white, beaten until frothy
few flaked almonds to decorate

Mix the coconut, ground rice and sugar in a bowl. Fold in the egg white with a metal spoon. Dampen your hands and take a heaped teaspoon of the mixture and form into a ball. Place the balls on a lightly greased baking tray. Press them lightly to flatten slightly and decorate them with a few flaked almonds.

Bake the macaroons for 12–15 minutes at 350°F / 180°C / Mark 4. Allow to cool on the baking tray for a minute or two, then slide a knife underneath to loosen them. Put the macaroons on a wire rack and when completely cold, store in an airtight tin.

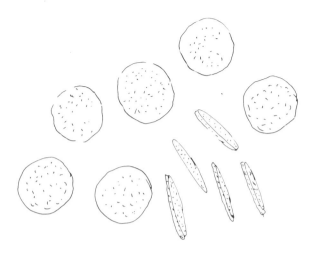

Bran Biscuits

Depending on whether you add yeast or malt extract, these biscuits are savoury or sweet.

Place the flour, baking powder and bran into a bowl. Add the margarine and rub in. Put the yeast or malt extract in a bowl with the milk and mix thoroughly. Add the egg and the milk mixture to the flour mixture, and stir with a fork to form a soft dough. Knead lightly with the fingertips.

Wrap the dough in a plastic bag and put into the refrigerator for 20 minutes. Heat the oven to 375°F / 190°C / Mark 5. Grease two baking sheets. Roll out the dough into a sausage shape and cut into slices ⅛ inch (3 mm) thick. Place the biscuits on baking sheets, and bake for 15–20 minutes, until golden brown.

7 oz / 225 g / 1¾ cups wholemeal flour
1 tsp baking flour
1 oz / 25 g / ¼ cup fine natural bran
4 oz / 125 g / ½ cup margarine
1 tsp yeast extract or 1 tsp malt extract
2 tbsp milk
1 beaten egg

Gooseberry Jam

Unripe gooseberries are better for jam as the skins are not so tough. Also, the jam will set more quickly because of the high pectin content. A test for setting and tips for bottling are given on page 16.

Top and tail the gooseberries. Put them in a large pan with the water and bring slowly to the boil. Mash them with a spoon and cook gently until tender. Add the sugar (pre-warmed), dissolve slowly and then bring to a rapid boil. Test for setting after 10 minutes. Have the jars, covers and labels ready. Let the jam stand a few minutes before bottling so that the fruit will be evenly distributed.

4 lb / 2 kg / 10½ cups unripe gooseberries
2 pints / 1½ litres / 5 cups water
6 lb / 3 kg / 16 cups Demerara sugar

JUNE

June finds the garden bursting forth. The fragrances of honeysuckle and roses waft through the open kitchen window. Your salad crops are beginning to be harvested, and you can switch off the stove and turn to the cooler pleasures of concocting endless varieties of delightful salads. These can make an appearance at any stage of a meal; as a starter, as an accompaniment to the main meal, or as the main meal itself. A good salad dressing is vital, of course (recipes, pages 75–76).

As an alternative to salads, I have included some cooked dishes using vegetables such as courgettes, marrows and tomatoes, all coming into season now. Try Summer Shepherds Pie (page 73) or Courgette Cutlets (page 74) for a light cooked meal.

On a hot day, fresh summer fruit is the obvious – and effortless! – choice for dessert. June is the start of the strawberry season, but leave bulk strawberry cooking until next month when the prices will be much lower, especially if you happen to live near a 'pick your own' farm.

This is the month that everyone starts getting busy with school fetes and fund-raising events, so I have added a few recipes for old favourites that always seem to sell well – toffee apples, gingerbread men, coconut biscuits and malt loaf. You may have to hide them away to ensure they reach the fete!

Your herbs will be at their best now and, as it is only a short season for most of them, it is a good idea to find ways of preserving them for use throughout the year. They can be hung in bunches in a cool airy place to dry, then the leaves stripped from the plants and put into airtight jars. Some are worth freezing, such as parsley, chives, sorrel and fennel. Their flavour seems better when frozen than dried. Thyme and tarragon sprigs added to bottles of cider vinegar enhance the flavour, making it delicious for salad dressings.

Lettuce Soup

2 tbsp butter or margarine
1 medium onion, finely chopped
1 large potato, peeled and diced
1½ pints / 90 cl / 4 cups vegetable stock
1 large lettuce, shredded
salt and pepper to taste
1 heaped tsp chopped mint

For this you can use lettuce that has blown. Everybody seems to get blown lettuce no matter how carefully you plan your planting.

Melt the butter or margarine in a large saucepan. Add the onion and sauté for 5 minutes. Add the potato and stir it around with the onion. Add the liquid, bring to the boil, then reduce the heat and simmer for 15 minutes. Add the lettuce leaves and simmer for 5 minutes. Take off the heat, allow to cool slightly, and then liquidize. Add seasoning and the mint. This soup is delicious served hot or cold.

Stuffed Tomatoes

6 good-sized tomatoes
5 oz / 150 g / 1¼ cups toasted chopped
    cashew nuts
1 large stick celery, finely chopped
pinch of cayenne pepper
6 oz / 175 g / ⅔ cup low-fat soft cheese
salt and pepper to taste

Slice the tops off the tomatoes and scoop out the flesh. Mix the flesh with the other ingredients. Stuff the centre of the tomatoes. Replace the tops and serve.

Fresh Tomato Soup

1 large onion, finely chopped
1 large carrot, grated
2 stalks celery, chopped
2 tbsp margarine
2 lb / 1 kg / 8 cups ripe chopped tomatoes
1 tsp basil
1 tsp oregano
2 pints / 1¼ litres / 5 cups vegetable stock
    (or 1 pint / 625 ml / 2½ cups stock and
    1 pint / 625 ml / 2½ cups milk for a
    creamier soup)
1 tbsp tomato purée
ground black pepper
1½ tsp salt

Fry the onion, carrot and celery in the margarine until transparent. Add the tomatoes, basil and oregano. Simmer for about 15 minutes until soft. Add the stock and cook for a further 10 minutes. Add the tomato purée, black pepper and salt. Allow to cool slightly, then liquidize or purée to make a smooth soup. Return the soup to the pan and reheat to serve.

Courgettes à la Grèque

Fry the onion and garlic in the oil for 5 minutes. Add the other ingredients and simmer for 10 minutes. Allow to cool and serve with good crusty bread to mop up the delicious juices.

1 large onion, sliced
1 clove garlic, crushed
2 tbsp olive oil
1¼ lb / 625 g / 4 cups sliced courgettes
¼ pint / 150 ml / ⅔ cup dry white wine
12 oz / 375 g / 3 cups peeled tomatoes, chopped

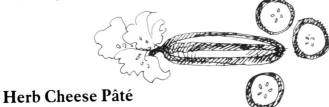

Herb Cheese Pâté

Put all the ingredients in a bowl together and beat until really smooth. Transfer to a pâté dish and chill until required. Serve with melba toast, crackers or good crusty bread.

1 lb / 500 g / 2 cups low-fat soft curd cheese
4 tbsp thick yogurt
1 tsp fresh chopped parsley
½ tsp fresh chopped chives
½ tsp fresh chopped sage
¼ tsp fresh chopped thyme
¼ tsp fresh chopped tarragon
¼ tsp fresh chopped mint
salt and pepper to taste
1 clove garlic, crushed
pinch of ground mace

Summer Shepherds Pie

Pod the broad beans. Sauté the onion in a little oil. Add the other vegetables (but not the potato!) and simmer in the pan, covering with a lid, for 15 minutes. Season and transfer to a 10 by 12 inch (25 by 30 cm) ovenproof dish. Spread the potato over the top. Sprinkle with the cheese. Bake for 15–20 minutes at 350°F / 180°C / Mark 4 until golden brown.

1 lb / 500 g / 3 cups broad beans (unpodded weight)
1 large onion, finely chopped
8 oz / 250 g / 4 cups sliced button mushrooms
1 lb / 500 g / 3 cups sliced carrots
1 lb / 500 g / 3 cups sliced fresh tomatoes
½ tsp dried basil or 1 tsp if fresh
salt and pepper to taste
2 lb / 1 kg / 7 cups mashed cooked potato
4 oz / 125 g / 1 cup grated Cheddar cheese

73

Courgette Cutlets

1 lb / 500 g / 3 cups sliced cooked courgettes
1 lb / 500 g / 3 cups mashed potato
2 onions, chopped and lightly fried
4 oz / 125 g / 1 cup grated cheese
salt and pepper to taste
1 tbsp fresh chopped parsley
½ tbsp fresh chopped mint
egg and breadcrumbs to coat

Mix all the ingredients together. Shape into cutlets. Roll the cutlets in the egg and breadcrumbs and fry in hot oil until each side is light golden brown.

Stuffed Marrow Flowers

1 bunch spring onions
2 cloves garlic
a little olive oil
8 oz / 250 g / 1 cup (dry weight) brown rice, cooked
5 tbsp tomato purée
1 tbsp fresh chopped parsley
½ tbsp fresh chopped fennel
½ tbsp fresh chopped mint
½ tsp ground cinnamon
salt and freshly ground pepper
24 marrow flowers
2 small beaten eggs
1 tsp lemon juice

If you grow your own marrows and courgettes, you will have plenty of spare flowers to make this recipe.

Finely chop the onions and garlic and fry them in the olive oil. Add the rice, 4 tbsp of tomato purée, herbs and seasoning. Cook for 2 or 3 minutes until well blended. Stuff each flower with this mixture, folding the petals over like a parcel. Place in an empty frying pan and cover with water, then simmer gently for about 25 minutes. Remove the parcels.

Stir the eggs, lemon juice and 1 tbsp tomato purée together in a bowl. Mix this into the stock in the pan and stir thoroughly. Replace the flowers in a pan and simmer for 5 minutes. Serve on a bed of brown rice (page 135).

Tomato Salad

Plunge the tomatoes into boiling water for a few seconds
and then skin them. Slice them across quite thickly.
Arrange on a large flat platter, overlapping the slices.
Mix the oil and vinegar together in a jar, shaking vigorously until thick. Season well with plenty of pepper and
salt. Sprinkle the basil and parsley over the tomatoes.
Carefully pour the dressing over. Leave for half an hour
for the tastes to combine, then serve.

1½ lb / 750 g / 8 firm ripe medium tomatoes
5 tbsp olive or sunflower oil
2 tbsp white wine vinegar
salt and pepper to taste
½ tbsp chopped fresh basil
1 tbsp parsley

Potato Salad

Peel the potatoes, boil until just tender, and cut into
cubes. Pour the dressing and herbs on while still hot.
Mix in the mayonnaise and shallot and serve.

2 lb / 1 kg / 5 cups sliced potatoes
¼ pint / 15 cl / ⅔ cup French dressing
   (below)
1 tsp chopped fresh chervil
1 tsp chopped fresh parsley
1 tsp chopped fresh tarragon
2 tbsp mayonnaise
1 tsp chopped fresh shallot

French Dressing

Put all the ingredients into a screw-top jar, cover and
shake vigorously. Store any unused dressing in the
refrigerator.

½ pint / 300 ml / 1⅓ cup vegetable oil
   (sunflower or olive are the nicest)
¼ pint / 150 ml / ⅔ cup cider vinegar
½ tsp dry mustard powder
salt and pepper to taste
pinch of paprika

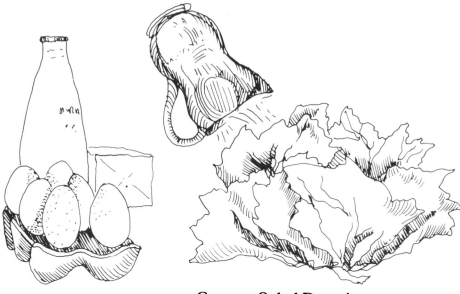

¼ pint / 150 ml / ⅔ cup milk
1 level tbsp unbleached white flour
1 level tsp English mustard powder
1 egg and 1 egg yolk
½ tbsp butter
2 tbsp cider vinegar
salt and pepper
4 or 5 tbsp milk, to dilute

1 large bunch mint
4 oz / 125 g / ⅔ cup Demerara sugar or
  honey
½ pint / 300 ml / 1⅓ cups cider vinegar

Creamy Salad Dressing

An easy salad dressing which is free from additives and inexpensive to make, this is for the members of the family who will not be converted to French dressing. Have all the ingredients at room temperature. Makes about ½ pint (300 ml) 1⅓ cups.

Put the milk, flour, mustard powder and eggs in a blender for 30 seconds. Pour the mixture into a pan and gradually bring to the boil, stirring all the time. Simmer for 2 minutes, then remove from the heat and stir in the butter, vinegar, salt and pepper. When cold, stir in enough milk to make a pouring consistency. Store the salad dressing in a jar or bottle in the refrigerator to improve its keeping qualities.

Mint Sauce

This is my son's favourite smothering for cabbage. Mint is one herb that grows wonderfully well with no trouble, apart from the fact that it is apt to travel all over the garden if not kept under check. It's worth growing it just to put in with new potatoes and peas!

Wash the mint thoroughly, then dry it and strip the leaves from the stalks. If you have a food processor, put the leaves in there to chop them finely. Otherwise, use a sharp knife. Transfer the mint to a bowl.

Dissolve the sugar in the vinegar in a saucepan over a low heat, then bring it to the boil. Pour this over the mint while it is still hot. Allow the sauce to get cold then bottle it. It will need dilution with vinegar before serving.

Toffee Apples

Heat the sugar, honey, vinegar, water and butter in a heavy-based saucepan. When the sugar has dissolved, boil rapidly for about 5 minutes to a temperature of 290°F / 143°C on a sugar thermometer, to the soft crack stage. If you do not have a thermometer, drop a little of the toffee into a bowl of cold water, and it should form threads which are hard, but not brittle. Push the sticks into the apples and dip them one at a time into the toffee. Stand on waxed paper to set. Wrap in waxed paper.

8 crispy apples, such as Red Delicious
8 oz / 250 g / 1⅓ cups Demerara sugar
8 oz / 250 g / ⅔ cup honey
2 tsp cider vinegar
¼ pint / 150 ml / ⅔ cup water
4 oz / 125 g / ½ cup butter
8 wooden sticks

Gingerbread Men

Melt the margarine, molasses and sugar in a saucepan. Sift the flour and spices together in a bowl. Stir the melted mixture into the flour until smooth. Take out of the bowl and roll into a piece about ¼ inch (6 mm) thick. Cut out gingerbread men (or women!) with your cutter. Bake for 10 minutes at 350°F / 180°C / Mark 3. Allow them to cool slightly then carefully transfer them to a wire rack. Store in an airtight tin.

4 oz / 125 g / ½ cup margarine
2 tbsp molasses
4 oz / 125 g / ⅔ cup medium Muscovado sugar
8 oz / 250 g / 2 cups plain wholemeal flour
1 tsp ground ginger
½ tsp cinnamon

Strawberry Whip

1½ lb / 750 g / 5 cups strawberries, stalks removed
4 oz / 125 g / ⅔ cup Demerara sugar
¼ tsp salt
5 egg whites
5 fl oz / 14 cl / 1 cup whipped double cream
few whole strawberries to decorate

Liquidize the strawberries with the sugar and salt. (Salt brings out the strawberries' flavour). Beat the egg whites until stiff and carefully fold them into the strawberries with a metal spoon. Fold in the whipped cream in the same way. Pour the whip into one large or six small serving dishes. Decorate with the remaining strawberries. Chill before serving.

Luxurious Strawberry Trifle

Madeira Cake Base
6 oz / 175 g / ¾ cup butter or margarine
6 oz / 175 g / 1 cup light Muscovado sugar
3 eggs, beaten
8 oz / 250 g / 2 cups 85% plain flour
1 tsp baking powder
¼ tsp salt

Custard
2 pints / 1¼ litres / 5 cups milk
6 tbsp Demerara sugar
6 eggs, beaten
½ tsp pure vanilla extract

Filling
12 fl oz / 500 ml / 1½ cups cream sherry or 4 fl oz / 125 g / 1 cup raspberry or strawberry liqueur
1½ lb / 750 g / 4½ cups strawberries, stalks removed

Topping
½ pint / 300 ml / 1⅓ cups whipped cream
strawberries to decorate

Make the cake a few days in advance as trifle is better with slightly stale cake.

For the cake, preheat the oven to 325°F / 170°C / Mark 3. Beat the butter and sugar together until light and fluffy. Add the beaten eggs using a little flour to prevent curdling. Sift in the remaining flour and baking powder and salt and mix in. Pour into a greased and lined 8 by 6 inch (20 by 16 cm) baking tin. Bake for 1–1¼ hours until golden and springy to the touch.

To make the custard, heat the milk and the sugar in a saucepan. Then, using a double saucepan or a bowl in the top of an ordinary pan, pour the milk, through a sieve, into the top pan or bowl. Pour in the eggs. Cook this over the saucepan of water until the mixture thickens. Remove from the heat and add the vanilla extract.

Assemble the trifle by putting the Madeira cake in the bottom of a glass serving dish. Pour the sherry or liqueur over the cake. Leave for a couple of minutes to soak in. Slice the strawberries over the cake and pour the cooled custard over the top. Refrigerate and, when completely cold, top with the whipped cream and strawberries.

Date and Ginger Cake

8 oz / 250 g / 2 cups 100% self-raising flour
¼ tsp salt
1 heaped tsp ground ginger
4 oz / 125 g / ½ cup margarine
2 oz / 60 g / ⅓ cup medium Muscovado
   sugar
4 oz / 125 g / ⅝ cup chopped dates
2 medium eggs
2 level tbsp malt extract
¼ pint / 150 ml / ⅔ cup milk
   (approximately)

Preheat the oven to 375°F / 190°C / Mark 5. Grease and line an 8 inch (20 cm) diameter cake tin. Sift the flour, ginger and salt together in a mixing bowl. Rub in the margarine, then stir in the sugar and dates. Beat the eggs well and add them to the mixture. Mix in the malt and enough milk to make a soft cake mixture. Pour into the cake tin. Bake for 40–45 minutes until firm and springy to the touch. Cool slightly, then turn out onto a wire rack.

Coconut Biscuits

4 oz / 125 g / ½ cup butter
4 oz / 125 g / ⅔ cup light Muscovado sugar
4 oz / 125 g / 1⅓ cups plain wholemeal flour
¼ tsp baking powder
4 oz desiccated coconut
1 large egg, beaten

Preheat the oven to 350°F / 180°C / Mark 4. Beat the sugar and butter together until light and fluffy. Sift in the flour, baking powder, and add the coconut. Add the egg to form a mixture pliable enough to be rolled out on a floured board. Use a pastry cutter, or cut into the desired shapes. Place on a baking sheet and bake for 20 minutes.

Malt Loaf

1 lb / 500 g / 4 cups wholemeal flour
½ tsp salt
8 oz / 250 g / 1¼ cups sultanas
1 oz / 30 g / 1 cake fresh yeast
¼ pint / 150 ml / ⅔ cup warm water
2 tbsp molasses
3 tbsp malt extract
2 tbsp margarine

Glaze
1 tbsp each of milk, water and Muscovado
   sugar

Preheat the oven to 400°F / 200°C / Mark 6. Mix the flour, salt and sultanas in a bowl. Dissolve the yeast in another small bowl with a little of the water. Allow it to froth up. In a saucepan, melt the molasses, malt and margarine. Allow to cool to hand heat, and then add to the flour mixture. Add the yeast. Knead thoroughly, and then cover with a plastic bag or damp cloth and allow to prove until almost double in size. Cut the dough in half and knead again, and place in two 1 lb (500 g) loaf tins. Allow to prove again. Bake until level with the top of tins, about 35–45 minutes. Melt the glaze in a saucepan, and paint over the loaves while they are still hot from the oven.

Peanut Cookies

These are a great favourite with children.

Preheat oven to 350°F / 180°C / Mark 4. Grease a large baking tray. Beat the sugar and butter together until light and creamy. Fold in the egg and peanut butter. Fold in the flour, and mix until smooth. Roll the mixture into little balls and place on the baking tray. Flatten them out slightly with a fork. Place a couple of peanuts on the top of each. Press in place. Bake for 12–15 minutes until golden brown. Cool on a wire rack. Store in a tin.

4 oz / 125 / ⅔ cup light Muscovado sugar
2 oz / 60 g / ¼ cup butter or margarine
1 medium egg
4 oz / 125 g / ½ cup crunchy peanut butter (page 62)
3 oz / 90 g / ¾ cup 85% self-raising flour
2 oz / 60 g / ½ cup whole peanuts

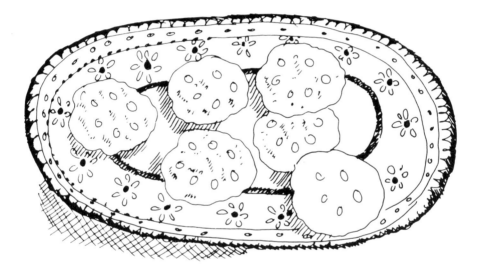

Carob Brownies

Preheat oven to 350°F / 180°C / Mark 4. Grease and line an 8 inch (20 cm) square baking tin. Melt the margarine and allow to cool. Sift the flour, baking powder, salt and carob powder into a bowl. Whisk the eggs and sugar together until light, fluffy and foamy, then fold in the flour and margarine. When blended, stir in the nuts and raisins. Spread the mixture into the baking tin and bake for about 25 minutes, until it is springy to the touch and the crust looks dull. Cut into squares, cool and serve.

2 oz / 60 g / ¼ cup vegetable margarine
3 oz / 80 g / ¾ cup plain wholemeal flour
1 level tsp baking powder
pinch salt
3 oz / 80 g / ¾ cup carob powder
2 large eggs
7 oz / 190 g / 1⅙ cup medium Muscovado sugar
4 oz / 125 g / 1 cup chopped walnuts
2 oz / 60 g / ⅓ cup raisins

JULY

This must be the month when there is the greatest proliferation of fruit and vegetables. The vegetable shops are full of bargains, so make the most of them by freezing and jam and wine making. The garden is at its height this month. There are still plenty of strawberries. Raspberries are at their cheapest. Vegetables include peas, beans, lettuce, carrots, tomatoes, beetroot and potatoes. Soft fruits are also plentiful.

With the children back home from school, it is a good idea to think ahead to give yourself plenty of time for excursions. There are ideas for food to take on picnics, suitable for the beach or park or woods. All children love a picnic, even if it is only on the lawn in the garden. If you are a working mother (and there are enough of us), it may be worth getting together with a friend and organizing trips on a share basis. This way your children get double treats.

It is surprising how much of interest there is to see locally. Libraries can give you details, and they also sometimes organize activities during the school vacation break, as do some enterprising schools. Older children could be interested in joining the Youth Hostel Association – in fact the whole family can join. It is a very inexpensive way of seeing the country and meeting people.

Scout and Guide Associations often take their members camping during summer months. If you feel like it, there is the American answer of sending your child away to summer camp. This idea is catching on over here. There are plenty of opportunities for playing all manner of sports – helpful if you have energetic youngsters on your hands. A few hours running on a tennis court will soon tire them out! Many large towns now have sports centres. These are a blessing as they combine all manner of sports and can cater for most needs.

Sorrel Soup

1 lb / 500 g / 16 cups washed sorrel leaves
2 small lettuce leaves
1 medium onion, finely chopped
2 tbsp butter or margarine
1¾ pints / 1 litre / 5 cups vegetable stock
salt and pepper
2 egg yolks
4 tbsp single cream

It is possible to find wild sorrel. Make sure you do not pick it directly from the roadside because of exhaust pollution.

Shred the sorrel and lettuce finely. Sauté the onion in the butter. Add the sorrel and lettuce and cook gently for a few minutes. Pour in the stock. Season to taste and simmer for about 10 minutes. Cool the mixture and then liquidize with the egg yolks. Stir in the cream to give a paler green colour. Chill. Serve decorated with thin cucumber slices.

Gazpacho

6 large ripe tomatoes
1 large cucumber
1 onion
1 medium green pepper
1¼ pints / 775 ml / 3⅙ cups tomato juice
4 tbsp olive oil
⅛ pint / 75 ml / 1 cup red wine vinegar
2 tbsp lemon juice
2 cloves garlic, crushed
dash Tabasco sauce
croutons to garnish (page 41)

This is the taste of summer in a soup bowl. It makes an excellent starter for a dinner party – you don't have to worry about it getting cold! It is also a great way of taking advantage of a glut of summer vegetables, because it freezes really well.

Dice some of the tomato, cucumber and onion for a garnish. Liquidize all the vegetables until smooth. Stir in the tomato juice and add the other ingredients, checking on the taste frequently. Season with salt and fresh ground pepper. Chill the soup before serving. Add a few ice cubes and the chopped vegetables in the serving dish. Top with croutons at the last minute.

Cream of Broad Bean Soup

1½ lb / 750 g / 4½ cups shelled broad beans
sprig of thyme
1 small onion, finely chopped
3 tbsp butter or margarine
1½ oz / 45 g / ⅓ cup flour
3 pints / 1250 ml / 7½ cups vegetable stock
5 fl oz / 140 ml / 1 cup double cream or top of
   the milk
3 tbsp chopped chervil (use parsley if
   chervil is not available)
salt and pepper to taste

Cook the beans in boiling water with the thyme for about 15 minutes. Drain the beans, reserving the liquid to be part of the stock. Fry the onion in the butter, stir in the flour, and cook for 3 minutes. Add the stock and bring to the boil. Simmer for 10 minutes. Add the beans to the stock and allow to cool slightly. Then liquidize and season to taste. Replace the soup in the saucepan and gently reheat, adding the cream and chervil. Check the seasoning and serve immediately.

Fennel Soup

Finely slice the fennel, reserving the feathery leaves for a garnish. Melt the butter in a large saucepan and add the fennel. Cook the fennel gently for 5 minutes. Add the flour and cook for 3 minutes, then gradually add the stock and season it. Bring to the boil, then simmer for 15 minutes. Allow to cool slightly and then liquidize. Return the soup to the pan and add the milk, stirring all the time. Swirl the cream onto the soup when it is in the bowls, with a sprinkling of chopped fennel leaves.

1 large bulb of fennel
2 oz / 60 g / ½ cup butter or margarine
1 oz / 30 g / ¼ cup plain flour
1½ pints / 925 ml / 3¾ cups vegetable stock
salt and pepper to taste
1½ pints / 925 ml / 3¾ cups milk
5 fl oz / 140 ml / 1 cup double cream (optional)

Beetroot and Tofu Dip

This dip has a beautiful colour.
   Mash the beetroot thoroughly. Cream the tofu with the seasoning and onion. Stir in the beetroot. Fill a pâté dish and serve with melba toast and crudités.

1 lb / 500 g / 3 cups freshly cooked beetroot, skinned
10 oz / 300 g / 2 cups packet soft tofu
1 tbsp finely chopped onion
½ tsp ground horseradish
salt and pepper to taste

Broad Bean Pâté

Melt the butter and sauté the onions for 3 minutes. Add the beans and peas. Cover the pan and allow them to cook in their own juice for about 10 minutes until tender. Stir in the herbs and cook for another 3 minutes. Remove from the heat and pound to a pulp. If you like really smooth pâté, put it through a food processor. Add salt and pepper to taste. Stir in the sherry, if using, and chill before serving.

2 oz / 60 g / ¼ cup butter
6 spring onions, finely chopped
1 lb / 500 g / 3 cups shelled broad beans
½ lb / 250 g / 1½ cups fresh shelled peas
1 tbsp chopped fennel leaf
2 tbsp fresh chopped parsley
salt and pepper
1 tbsp cooking sherry (optional)

Ratatouille

Put the aubergine and courgettes into a colander and sprinkle them with salt. Leave to stand for half an hour then rinse under cold water and drain. Fry the onion and garlic in the oil gently. Add the red peppers, courgettes, aubergines, tomatoes and herbs. Season well. Simmer, covered, for about 30 minutes. Serve hot or cold with crusty break to soak up the delicious juices. This is a perfect dish to serve at barbecues, as you can make it well in advance.

1 large aubergine in 1 inch (2.5 cm) slices
3 medium courgettes in 1 inch (2.5 cm) slices
2 medium onions, chopped
2 cloves garlic, crushed
4 tbsp olive oil
2 medium red peppers, deseeded and sliced
6 large tomatoes, skinned, quartered and deseeded
1 tsp dried basil
a pinch oregano
salt and pepper

Stuffed Baked Aubergines

4 large aubergines
1 large onion, finely chopped
1 green pepper, deseeded and chopped
2 cloves garlic, crushed
1¼ lb / 625 g / 5 cups sliced ripe tomatoes
4 oz / 125 g / ⅔ cup red kidney beans,
   soaked overnight
¼ tsp dried basil or 1 tsp fresh basil
3 tbsp parsley
pepper and salt to taste
3 oz / 75 g / ¾ cup grated Cheddar cheese
1 oz / 25 g / ¼ cup grated Parmesan

Cut the aubergines in half lengthways. Scoop out the flesh and dice it. Sprinkle the shells with salt and leave to stand for half an hour to draw out moisture. Rinse them and drain. Heat a little oil in a pan and fry the onion until soft. Add the green pepper, garlic, diced aubergine and tomatoes and fry for 5 minutes. Cook the aubergine shells in boiling water for 2 minutes and then drain. Mix the beans and herbs in with the vegetables and season. Spoon in the filling, sprinkle with the cheese and bake at 375°F / 190°C / Mark 5 for 25 minutes; serve.

Macaroni Stir Fry

Have all the vegetables assembled together ready to cook. Cook the macaroni for 10 minutes in boiling salted water. Drain. Heat 1 tbsp oil in a large pan or wok. Add the onion, ginger and garlic and cook them until soft. Remove from the pan. Add another tablespoon of oil, and add the remaining vegetables. Return the onion, ginger and garlic with the macaroni to the pan. Mix the arrowroot and soy sauce together in a small basin. Add to the pan with 1 pint / 60 cl / 2½ cups water. Season to taste, then cook for a further 3 minutes. Serve immediately.

12 oz / 375 g / 2 cups wholewheat macaroni
1 large onion, finely chopped
1 inch (2.5 cm) piece ginger, freshly grated
1 clove garlic, crushed
1 lb / 500 g / 3 cups broad beans
6 oz / 175 g / 1 cup thinly sliced green pepper
6 oz / 175 g / ½ cup sliced courgettes
6 oz / 175 g / ¾ cup thinly sliced carrots
3 oz / 85 g / ½ cup French beans, snapped into pieces
3 oz / 85 g / ½ cup white cabbage, shredded
3 tsp arrowroot
5 tbsp soy sauce
salt and freshly ground pepper to taste

Watercress and Mushroom Quiche

Shortcrust Pastry
4 oz / 125 g / 1 cup self-raising wholewheat
  flour
4 oz / 125 g / 1 cup plain wholewheat flour
4 oz / 125 g / ½ cup vegetable margarine
pinch salt
about 4 tbsp cold water

Filling
1 fresh bunch watercress (kept upside down
  in a bowl of water until you use it)
4 oz / 125 g / 2 cups button mushrooms
3 eggs
½ pint / 300 ml / 1⅓ cups creamy milk
salt and pepper to taste
4 oz / 125 g / 1 cup grated Cheddar cheese
pinch ground mace

Mix the fat into the flour and salt quickly with your fingertips. Do not over-rub as you will make it greasy and the pastry will be liable to be a bit hard. It should resemble fine breadcrumbs. Cut the water in a little at a time with a knife. Make the pastry a little wetter than you think it should be as it absorbs water while it is resting. Having it dry means you will never be able to roll it out in one piece and transfer it to your flan dish.

After the pastry has rested – about an hour in the fridge is ideal – roll it out on a floured board. The colder you can keep the pastry the better. A marble slab is ideal for rolling out on, but you will have to make sure to flour it well. Line a 10 inch (22 cm) flan ring or flan tin with the rolled out pastry. Prick the flan case and bake for 10 minutes at 425°F / 220°C / Mark 7. Allow to cool.

For the filling, slice the mushrooms thinly and spread them in the flan case, reserving a few for the top. Drain and dry the watercress. Mix the other ingredients together in a bowl. Pour over the vegetables and bake for about 40 minutes at 375°F / 190°C / Mark 5 until set and golden. Serve hot or cold.

Spanish-Style Chick Peas

1 lb / 500 g / 2⅔ cups chick peas (soaked for
  at least 24 hours)
2 bay leaves
1 large onion, roughly chopped
1 large carrot, sliced
1 stick celery, roughly chopped
1 large clove garlic, crushed
2 lb / 1 kg / 16 cups ripe tomatoes, chopped
2 tbsp tomato purée
1 tbsp fresh chopped parsley
1 tbsp fresh thyme (¼ tbsp if dried)
salt and pepper to taste

Drain the chick peas and cover with fresh water. Add the bay leaves and cook for at least 2 hours until soft. Drain the chick peas, reserving 1 pint / 600 ml / 2⅔ cups of the liquid to put in the casserole dish with them. Sauté the chopped vegetables in a little oil to soften them. Put these into a large casserole with the chick peas. Mix the tomato purée with the reserved stock then season it and add to the casserole. Stir in the remaining ingredients. Cover with a lid and place in a 325°F / 170°C / Mark 3 oven for 1½ to 2 hours until thick and well cooked.

Beetroot and Onion Salad

1 lb / 500 g / 3 cups cooked beetroot
6 spring onions
2 tbsp orange juice
3 tbsp olive oil
salt and pepper
¼ tsp dry mustard powder

Chop the beetroot and spring onion bulbs (use the green parts as a garnish in another dish). Mix the remaining ingredients together in a screw-top jar, shaking well. Toss the dressing into the onion and beetroot.

Fennel and Avocado Salad

Combine the fennel with the lettuce in the bottom of a shallow serving dish. Arrange the oranges over the top. Peel the avocados and slice them thinly. Arrange these in the dish. Pour the French dressing over the top, and serve at once.

1 large head of fennel, shredded
1 large lettuce, shredded
3 oranges, peeled and sliced
2 large avocado pears
¼ pint / 150 ml / ⅔ cup French dressing (page 75)

Beetroot and Horseradish Relish

Peel the beetroot and chop it into cubes. Stir it into the horseradish. Add the sugar and salt. Mix thoroughly and put into jars. Top up the jars with the vinegar. This can be used at once and will keep about one month.

P.S. Adding a pinch of ground horseradish to pickled beetroot will prevent mould forming.

1 lb / 500 g / 3 cups cooked beetroot
¼ lb / 125 g / 1 cup grated horseradish (don swimming goggles and scarf tied around your mouth before starting; this beats peeling onions as a tear jerking job!)
4 oz / 125 g / ⅔ cup Demerara sugar
1 tsp salt
½ pint / 300 ml / 1¼ cups white wine vinegar

Creamy Soya Dressing

Warm the soya milk slightly in a saucepan and pour it into a blender. Gradually add the oil, a little at a time to prevent curdling. Blend until thick. Pour into a bowl, and mix in the other ingredients. Keep refrigerated in glass jars or bottles until needed.

½ pint / 300 ml / 1⅓ cups unsweetened soya milk
1 pint / 600 ml / 2½ cups olive or sunflower oil
1 tbsp medium Muscovado sugar (optional – if preferred, you can use the pre-sweetened soya milk)
2 tbsp cider vinegar
1 heaped tsp prepared English mustard
1 tsp salt
ground pepper

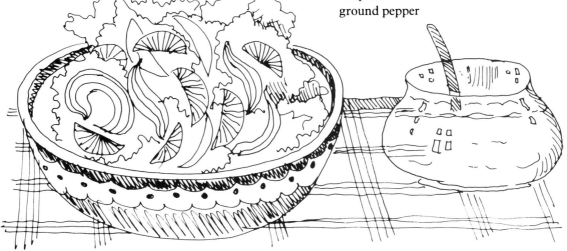

Strawberry and Rhubarb Pie

Pie Crust
6 oz / 175 g / ¾ cup butter
8 oz / 250 g / 2 cups plain flour

Filling
3 oz / 80 g / ¾ cup ground almonds
12 oz / 375 g / 2½ cups strawberries
8 oz / 250 g / 1¾ cups cooked rhubarb
8 oz / 250 g / 1⅓ cups Demerara sugar
1½ oz / 45 g / ⅓ cup plain flour
pinch salt
2 tbsp butter or margarine
milk and a little sugar to glaze the top

Rub the butter into the flour quickly. Add enough water to make a soft dough – about 4 tablespoons. Divide the pastry in half, and roll out a piece to line the bottom and a piece for the pie crust. Line a 9 inch (22 cm) pie dish and bake the base blind for 10 minutes at 375°F / 190°C / Mark 5.

Sprinkle the pie base with the ground almonds. Mix all the other ingredients, excluding the butter, together and place in the pie case. Dot with the butter. Damp the edges of the pie case and put on the lid. Crimp the edges. Brush with the milk and sprinkle with the sugar to glaze the top. Bake at the set temperature for 45 minutes.

Raspberry and Redcurrant Fool

This is an old English sweet dish made with fresh fruit and cream, but I have used yogurt to make it lower in cholesterol. Cream can be used if you prefer.

Wash and dry the raspberries and redcurrants. Put them into a basin and cook over a pan of boiling water until they are soft – about 30 minutes. Crush the berries through a sieve and stir them into the yogurt, then sweeten with a little sugar, if you wish. Spoon the fool into serving dishes and garnish with the reserved redcurrants.

1 lb / 500 g / 3 cups raspberries
4 oz / 125 g / 1 cup redcurrants plus a few for
  decoration
¾ pint / 450 ml / 2 cups thick yogurt
sugar to sweeten, if desired

Strawberry Jam

4 lb / 2 kg / 13 cups strawberries
juice of 1 lemon
4 lb / 2kg / 10 cups Demerara sugar

Use strawberries that are slightly underripe as they contain more pectin. Hull the strawberries and place them in a large pan with the lemon juice. Cook gently until soft. Add the warmed sugar and stir over a low heat until the sugar dissolves. Bring to the boil, and boil rapidly for about 20–25 minutes until setting point is reached. Test for set either with a sugar thermometer or with a little jam on a saucer, drawing your finger over the surface to see if it wrinkles. Remove any scum from the top. Leave the jam in the saucepan for about half an hour before potting. This helps prevent the strawberries from rising to the surface in the jars. Pot the jam (page 16) and label the jars. Store in a cool, dry place.

Raspberry Jam

4 lb / 2 kg / 13 cups raspberries
4 lb / 2 kg / 10 cups Demerara sugar

Use the same method as for the strawberry jam above, cooking the raspberries gently in their own juice.

Rhubarb and Blackcurrant Jam

Cut the rhubarb into 1 inch (2.5 cm) pieces. Strip the blackcurrants from their stems. Put the fruit into a pre-serving pan, add the water, and simmer for about 40 minutes until the fruit is soft. Add the sugar, and stir over a low heat until dissolved. Bring to the boil, and boil rapidly until the setting point is reached. Remove from the heat, and remove the scum. Bottle the jam (page 16).

1 lb / 500 g / 3 cups rhubarb
2 lb / 1 kg / 6 cups blackcurrants
¾ pint / 450 ml / 2 cups water
3½ lb / 1.75 kg / 9⅓ cups Demerara sugar

Blackcurrant Liqueur

Start this now and you will have a special drink to offer your friends at Christmas.

Pour the brandy into a large, wide-necked jar – such as a large glass candy jar – which you have sterilized. Crush the fruit slightly. Stir the sugar into the brandy, pour in the fruit and seal the jar tightly. Shake the jar regularly every few days or so for the first month. Leave to stand in a dark, dry place for at least another two months. After this time, filter it into sterilized bottles.

1 lb / 500 g / 4 cups blackcurrants
2 pints / 1250 ml / 5 cups brandy
4 oz / 125 g / ⅔ cup Demerara sugar

AUGUST

August sees the children still on school holidays. The weather is usually good, and the days very long. It is pleasant to be able to eat alfresco, and it is a delightful way to entertain – no worrying about crumbs on the carpet.

If you have children with birthdays this month, the garden is the place for a party. Pitch a tent in which to lay out the food, set up some music, and you have the ingredients for success. The same set up can apply to adults; they love a barbecue. With more and more people turning part of their garden over to patios, so there is somewhere to sit and place a table, to organize a barbecue is relatively easy.

You can entertain quite a large group of people without missing the fun by having to keep dashing to the kitchen between courses, as you would with a dinner party. Grill Vegetable Kebabs (page 97), serve platters of interesting salads (Cucumber and Strawberry; and Coconut Rice, page 100) and make a selection of non-alcoholic summer drinks (page 104) and you can't go wrong.

There are many imported fruits and vegetables in the shops this month; together with your home-grown produce, this is a bonanza month. Freeze all you can, either on its own or as part of a prepared meal to save time later. Get your preserving pans out and make the most of cheap apricots, peaches and pineapples. Blackcurrants and raspberries are still plentiful. The chances of buying the more unusual fruits such as redcurrants and loganberries get slimmer.

The high cost of labour to pick soft fruit means fewer and fewer commercial growers. The pick-your-own farms seem to be your best bet nowadays. It can be quite a nice day out for the family, and with everyone picking together, you will soon get all you need for a giant jam-making session (recipes, page 92).

Cucumber Soup

3 large cucumbers, peeled and coarsely
    chopped
1 large clove garlic
½ onion, finely chopped
3 tbsp unbleached white flour
1 pint / 625 ml / 2½ cups vegetable stock
1 tsp salt
5 fl oz / 140 ml / 1 cup sour cream or yogurt
½ tbsp fresh chopped dill
pinch ground mace
thin slices of cucumber and thinly pared
    lemon rind to garnish

Sauté the garlic and onion in a little oil for 3 minutes. Add the cucumber and sauté for a further 5 minutes. Stir in the flour, and add the stock and salt. Bring to the boil and simmer for 10 minutes. Cool slightly, then liquidize. Add the cream, dill and mace. Cool thoroughly before serving, garnished with the cucumber and lemon rind.

Artichoke and Hazelnut Soup

1 large onion, finely chopped
2 oz / 60 g / ¼ cup butter or margarine
2 lb / 1 kg / 6 cups peeled and sliced
    Jerusalem artichokes
1 oz / 30 g / ¼ cup flour
1 pint / 625 ml / 2½ cups vegetable stock
4 oz / 125 g / 1 cup hazelnuts
salt and pepper to taste
1 pint / 625 ml / 2½ cups milk
a few hazelnuts, chopped for garnish

Sauté the onion in the butter. Add the artichokes and cook for 3 minutes. Stir in the flour and cook for 1 minute. Gradually stir in the stock. Cover the pan and simmer for 15 minutes until the artichokes are cooked. Allow to cool slightly, then liquidize with the whole hazelnuts. Return the soup to the pan and season. Stir in the milk, and gently reheat to serve. Decorate with the chopped nuts. This soup can be served cold or hot.

Baked Sweetcorn

6 fresh cobs of corn
2 onions, finely chopped
2 green peppers, sliced
5 oz / 140 g / ½ cup tomato purée
½ pint / 30 cl / 1¼ cups vegetable stock
4 oz / 125 g / 1 cup grated Cheddar cheese
4 oz / 125 g / 2 cups wholemeal breadcrumbs
½ tsp cayenne pepper
salt and pepper to taste

Cut the corn from the cobs. Sauté the onions and green peppers in a little oil. Add the tomato purée and vegetable stock. Cover and simmer for 3 minutes. Add the corn, and simmer for a further 5 minutes to tenderize. Transfer the mixture to a casserole dish. Mix the cheese and breadcrumbs together, then mix in the cayenne and season. Sprinkle the cheese mixture over the vegetables. Bake for 20 minutes at 350°F / 175°C / Mark 4.

Parsley Eggs

Divide the cottage cheese between six serving dishes. Place two halves of hard-boiled egg on each one. In a screw-top jar, place the other ingredients and shake thoroughly. Pour the dressing over the eggs, and serve.

6 hard-boiled eggs, halved
6 oz / 180 g / ¾ cup cottage cheese
dash soya sauce
⅓ tsp dry mustard powder
18 olives, pitted
1½ tsp lemon juice
1½ tsp clear honey
1 tbsp chopped fresh parsley
salt and pepper to taste

Vegetable Kebabs

Serve these with barbecue sauce and brown rice or on their own as part of your barbecue.

Thread the vegetables on to six skewers. Grill for 10 minutes, turning occasionally to brown. You can reheat them over your barbecue.

To make the sauce, blend the arrowroot with a little water. Put the other ingredients into a pan and heat them up. Stir the arrowroot in. Bring to the boil and simmer until thickened. Pour into a dish for spooning over the kebabs.

6 small, sweet firm tomatoes
6 button tomatoes
12 slices courgette
1 small red pepper, cut into 6 slices
6 pieces onion
6 pineapple chunks

Barbecue Sauce
1 tbsp arrowroot
1 clove garlic, crushed
1 tsp grated fresh ginger
1 tsp honey
1 tbsp sherry
squeeze of tomato purée
3 tbsp soya sauce

Cous-Cous and Summer Vegetables

4 carrots, grated
3 onions, finely chopped
3 sticks celery
4 oz / 125 g / 1 cup broad beans
1 broccoli spear
4 oz / 125 g / 1 cup sweetcorn
14 oz / 400 g / 2 cups canned tomatoes
4 oz / 125 g / 1 cup chopped pine kernels
3 oz / 75 g / 1½ cups wholemeal
  breadcrumbs
4 oz / 125 g / ¾ cup cous-cous
3 beaten eggs
3 tbsp lemon juice
3 tbsp each chopped parsley and basil
1 pint / 500 ml / 2½ cups vegetable stock

Cook the vegetables in boiling water for 5 minutes. Reserve the liquid for the vegetable stock. Mix the nuts, breadcrumbs, cous-cous and eggs together in a bowl. Add the strained vegetables, lemon juice and herbs and mix together. Pour the mixture into a large, lidded casserole dish. Pour on the stock and bake at 350°F / 175°C / Mark 4 for 40 minutes.

Stuffed Peppers

Plunge the peppers into boiling water for 3 minutes. Cut off the stalk ends to make lids. Deseed them and leave to cool while you make the stuffing. Heat a little oil in a pan and sauté the onion and garlic. Add the tomatoes and tomato purée, and cook until soft and mushy. Stir in the herbs, rice, nuts and cheese. Season to taste. Stuff each of the peppers with the mixture. Pop the lids on the peppers and place them in a baking dish. Pour a little water in the bottom. Bake the peppers at 375°F / 190°C / Mark 5 for 35–45 minutes, or until tender.

6 large peppers (try to pick squat ones as they balance better and are easier to fill)
1 large onion, chopped
1 clove garlic, crushed
12 oz / 375 g / 3 cups tomatoes, chopped
1 tbsp tomato purée
½ tsp each dried basil and oregano
6 oz / 180 g / ¾ cup cooked brown rice
3 oz / 80 g / ¾ cup finely chopped cashew nuts
4 oz / 125 g / 1 cup grated Cheddar cheese

Savoury Eggs

Mix the dry ingredients together. Stir in the vegetable stock and seasoning. Allow the mixture to stand for half an hour, then divide it into 6 pieces, and mould around the eggs. Brush with egg, and roll in the breadcrumbs. Heat some oil, and fry the eggs until they are golden brown. Drain them on kitchen paper.

6 hard-boiled eggs
8 oz / 250 g / 2 cups ground cashews
5 oz / 125 g / 2 cups breadcrumbs
2 tbsp soya flour
4 tbsp oatflakes
2 tsp basil
3 fl oz / 90 ml / ⅓ cup vegetable stock
salt and pepper
beaten egg and breadcrumbs to coat

Pineapple and Beansprout Salad

12 oz / 375 g / 2⅓ cups fresh pineapple, cut
   into cubes
8 oz / 250 g / 4 cups mung beansprouts
8 oz / 250 g / 2 cups Edam cheese, cubed
8 oz / 250 g ⅓ 2 cups carrots, grated
salt

Dressing
4 tbsp crunchy peanut butter
1 tbsp clear honey
4 tsp soya sauce
ground black pepper

Mix the pineapple, beansprouts, cheese and carrots together in a bowl and season. In a screw-top jar, shake the dressing ingredients vigorously until well blended. Pour the dressing over the prepared salad.

Cucumber and Strawberry Salad

1 large cucumber, peeled and thinly sliced
8 oz / 250 g / 1¾ cups strawberries, hulled
   and sliced
salt and pepper to taste
2 tbsp white wine vinegar
1 tsp Demerara sugar
chopped chives or spring onion to garnish

As the strawberry season comes to an end, here is a delicious starter to provide a reminder of the taste of Summer.

Arrange the cucumber and strawberries on a flat dish and season well. Mix the wine vinegar and sugar, and pour over the top. Sprinkle with the chives. Cover with plastic wrap and refrigerate until you are ready to serve.

Coconut Rice Salad

8 oz / 250 g / 1 cup brown rice plus 2 tsp
   curry powder
salt and pepper
2 level tbsp creamed coconut
2 oz / 60 g / ⅜ cup diced cucumber
¼ onion or shallot, very finely chopped
½ small pineapple, cored and chopped
2 oz / 60 g / ½ cup roughly chopped
   hazelnuts

Cook the rice with the curry powder in boiling salted water for 35 to 40 minutes, until just tender. Stir in ground pepper and creamed coconut while the rice is still hot. Cool completely. Add the cucumber, onion, pineapple and hazelnuts. Transfer the salad to a serving dish or, for a special effect, press the mixture into a ring mould and chill for at least 20 minutes before turning out.

Deep Fruit Tart

Rub the margarine into the flour. Add enough water to make a soft dough – about 4 tablespoons. Roll out the pastry and use it to line an 8 inch (20 cm) round cake tin – one with a loose bottom is best but not crucial. Bake blind for 15 minutes at 400°F / 200°C / Mark 6. Allow the pastry case to cool completely, then take it out of the tin.

Dissolve the arrowroot in a little water. Pour the orange juice into a saucepan, stir in the arrowroot, and cook for 2 or 3 minutes until thick and clear. Allow to cool. Spread a little of this mixture over the bottom of the flan case. Chill it until set. Arrange the fruit in the pastry case. Spoon the remaining arrowroot mixture over the fruit. Cool and serve.

8 oz / 250 g / 2 cups wholemeal flour
4 oz / 125 g / ½ cup margarine
1 oz / 30 g / ¼ cup arrowroot
½ pint / 315 ml / 1¼ cups orange juice
2 apples, peeled, cored and sliced
2 oranges, peeled and segmented
2 peaches, peeled, stoned and sliced
12 strawberries, cut into halves
½ fresh pineapple, peeled and thinly sliced
2 bananas, sliced

Caribbean Bananas

Bake the bananas in their skins at 325°F / 170°C / Mark 3 for 30 minutes, until the skins are black. Peel them carefully and place in a serving dish. Mix the other ingredients together and pour over the top. Sprinkle a few coconut strands on top to decorate.

6 bananas
4 tbsp light Muscovado sugar
juice of 3 limes
1 oz / 30 g / ⅓ cup coarse cut desiccated coconut
8 fl oz / 250 ml / 1¼ cups double cream or thick yogurt

101

Pineapple and Hazelnut Pudding

1 small pineapple, cored and peeled
3 oz / 75 g / ¾ cup toasted hazelnuts
6 oz / 150 g / ¾ cup vegetable margarine
6 oz / 150 g / 1 cup light Muscovado sugar
3 eggs
6 oz / 150 g / 1½ cups 85% self-raising flour

Grease and line a 2 lb (1 kg) pudding basin. Slice the pineapple into rings. Grind all but 9 of the hazelnuts. Place 3 pineapple rings in the bottom of the basin and put a hazelnut in the centre of each. Beat the margarine and sugar together until creamy. Beat in the eggs. Use a little of the ground hazelnut to prevent curdling. Add the remaining hazelnut and flour. Pour half the mixture on top of the pineapple in the basin. Top with the remaining fruit and nuts. Pour the remaining mixture over this. Tie wax paper or tin foil on top of the basin. Put into a pan of boiling water and steam for 2 hours.

Apricot Bakewell Tart

1 lb / 500 g / 3 cups fresh apricots
12 oz / 375 g / 2 cups flour
½ cup margarine
3 tbsp apricot jam
4 oz / 125 g / ½ cup vegetable margarine
4 oz / 125 g / ⅔ cup light Muscovado sugar
1 oz / 30 g / ¼ cup 85% self-raising flour
2 medium eggs
4 oz / 125 g / 1 cup ground almonds
1 tsp almond extract
few flaked almonds for decoration.

Rub the margarine into the flour. Add enough water to make a soft dough – about 4 tbsp. Roll it out and use to line a 9 inch (22 cm) flan tin. Simmer the apricots in a little water until cooked. Spread the jam on the pastry.

Beat the margarine and sugar together until light and fluffy. Add the flour and eggs, beating them into the flour. Stir in the ground almonds and almond extract. Pour onto the jam carefully. Bake in the oven at 350°F / 180°C / Mark 4 for 20 minutes. Arrange the apricots on top of the tart and sprinkle with the almond flakes, then bake for another 10–15 minutes until set and golden.

Courgette Cake

10 oz / 310 g / 1⅔ cups light Muscovado
   sugar
8 oz / 250 g / 1 cup vegetable margarine
3 beaten eggs
10 oz / 310 g / 2½ cups 85% self-raising flour
1 tsp ground cinnamon
1 tsp ground nutmeg
1 lb / 500 g / 3 cups grated courgettes
6 oz / 185 g / 1½ cups chopped walnuts

Beat the sugar and margarine together until they are light and fluffy. Beat in the eggs, adding a little flour to prevent curdling. Stir in the remaining flour and spices. Stir in the courgettes and walnuts. Mix well. Pour into a greased and lined 2 lb (1 kg) loaf tin. Bake for about 1¼–1½ hours at 350°F / 180°C / Mark 4. Allow the cake to cool slightly before turning it out.

Peach Chutney

This will make about 8 lb / 4 kg of chutney.

Mince the onions, raisins and apples. Add them to a large pan with the chopped peaches. Add all the other ingredients except the sugar, and simmer until soft. Add the sugar, and dissolve over a low heat. Continue to simmer until thick and there is no liquid to be seen. Pot the chutney (page 16). Store in a cool, dark place.

3 lb / 1½ kg / 12 cups chopped onions
¾ lb / 375 g / 1¾ cups raisins
2 lb / 1 kg / 12½ cups chopped apples
4 lb / 2 kg / 11¼ cups peaches, stoned and cut into pieces
1 tsp dry mustard powder
1 tsp chilli powder
2 tsp salt
juice and rind of 1 orange and 1 lemon
1 tsp turmeric
1 tsp ground cinnamon
1 pint / 625 ml / 2½ cups cider vinegar
1 lb / 500 g / 2⅔ cups light Muscovado sugar

Peach Jam

This will make about 5 lb / 2.5 kg of jam. Techniques for testing the setting point of jam and bottling it are on page 16.

Remove the stones from the peaches, roughly chop them, then put them in a pan with the water and lemon juice. Simmer until soft. Add the warmed sugar and heat gently to dissolve. Bring to the boil and continue to boil until setting point is reached. This will take about 20 minutes. Test the jam for setting. Cool the jam slightly and bottle it.

4 lb / 2 kg / 15 cups peaches, slightly underripe are best
juice of 2 lemons
¼ pint / 150 ml / ⅔ cup water
3½ lb / 1¾ kg / 9⅓ cups Demerara sugar

Long, hot days call for long, cool drinks. Here are a few ideas for some non-alcoholic drinks to serve with your barbecue, or to quench your thirst at any time.

Pineapple Punch

1 pineapple, peeled, cored and finely chopped
1½ pints / 90 cl / 4 cups pure pineapple juice
¾ pint / 45 cl / 2 cups orange juice
1½ pints / 90 cl / 4 cups ginger ale
crushed ice to taste

Mix all the ingredients except for the ice together in a large bowl. Add the crushed ice just before serving.

Strawberry Milkshake

1½ lb / 750 g / 5 cups fresh strawberries
3 pints / 1¾ litres / 8 cups milk
3 tsp honey
mint leaves to decorate

Put the strawberries, milk and honey in a liquidizer and blend for about 1 minute. You may need to do this in a couple of lots depending on the size of your liquidizer. Pour the milkshake into tall glasses and decorate with the mint leaves.

Homemade Lemonade

This is so much tastier than the commercial version and is very inexpensive to make. It is a good idea to always have some in the fridge in hot weather as it is an ideal thirstquenching drink.

Scrub the lemons and thinly pare the rind off with a potato peeler. Cut the lemons into pieces and put them into a large saucepan, with the lemon rinds, sugar and boiling water. Boil for 15 minutes. Allow to cool, strain and serve.

6 lemons
2 lb / 1 kg / 5⅓ cups sugar
3 pints / 1¾ litres / 8 cups boiling water

Iced Coffee

Mix the coffee with the boiling water in a large jug. Add the sugar and vanilla pod and allow to infuse. When needed for serving remove the vanilla pod and add the cold milk. Pour into six tall glasses, top with scoops of the ice cream, and sprinkle with the cinnamon and chocolate.

6 tbsp coffee granules (preferably decaffeinated)
1 pint / ⅔ litre / 2½ cups boiling water
4 oz / 125 g / ⅔ cup light brown sugar
1 vanilla pod
3 pints / 2 litres / 8 cups cold milk
Block of vanilla ice cream
3 tbsp grated chocolate mixed with 1 teaspoon cinnamon

SEPTEMBER

September is the traditional month of the harvest, when the abundance of fruit and vegetables is gathered and stored for the coming winter months. Historically, food preservation was essential to survival; nowadays we preserve food by freezing, bottling and careful storage to take advantage of cheap and plentiful produce. By doing this, we provide ourselves with out-of-season foods far superior to the goods available in supermarkets.

As well as produce from your garden, there is a wide variety of wild fruits and berries to be found in the fields and hedgerows. You can take the children out blackberry picking as there are still a couple of weeks in September before they have to go back to school. If the weather is warm enough, combine this excursion with a late-summer picnic. There are wild roses growing still in places where you can gather the rosehips to make rosehip syrup (page 129), an invaluable source of Vitamin C to help guard against winter colds. Other things available are chestnuts, sloes, rowan berries, elderberries, damsons and crab apples.

Some of the garden produce coming to fruition now are plums, apples, runner beans, marrows, and onions, and there are usually large amounts of unripened tomatoes for green tomato chutney.

So the next two months should be a busy time in the kitchen, as you make preserves, chutneys and jams for the Christmas period and to see you through the coming year.

It is still possible to pick field mushrooms in September. It is a good idea to have a handbook to refer to if you are picking mushrooms and other fungi. There are countless edible varieties. On the continent, they are more adventurous when it comes to eating fungi. Try out a few – but check your facts first!

Sweetcorn Soup

1½ lb / 750 g / 5 cups cooked sweetcorn
   kernels
¾ pint / 450 ml / 2 cups vegetable stock
2 tbsp butter
1 small onion
1 level tbsp flour
1 pint / 625 ml / 2½ cups milk
1 tsp salt
2–3 tbsp single cream
fresh ground pepper
chopped parsley to garnish

Add the stock to the sweetcorn, and simmer for 20 minutes. Take off the heat, cool slightly, and then liquidize. Melt the butter, and fry the onion in it until it is soft. Stir in the flour. Add the onion to the sweetcorn mixture, season, bring to the boil, and then reduce the heat, add the milk and simmer for 2 or 3 minutes. Take from the heat, and stir in the cream. Sprinkle with the parsley to serve.

Avocado and Pear Starter

3 avocado pears
3 William pears
lettuce leaves for serving
juice of 1 lemon
3 tbsp double cream
6 oz / 165 g / ¾ cup low-fat cream cheese
a little French dressing (page 75)

Place the lettuce leaves on six serving dishes. Cut the avocados in half, and take out the stones. Peel the skin away, and cut the flesh into thin slices. Peel the William pears, core, and slice fairly thinly. Sprinkle the lemon juice over the pears. In a fan shape, place alternate slices of the pears on the beds of lettuce. Mix the cream and cheese together and place a small mound at the base of the fans. Drizzle the French dressing over the pears. Garnish with a couple of slices of tomato to add a little colour.

Tabbouleh

12 oz / 375 g / 2 cups bulgar wheat
1 onion, finely chopped
¼ pint / 150 ml / ⅔ cup cold pressed olive
   oil
4 tbsp lemon juice
1 large bunch parsley, finely chopped
2 oz / 60 g / 1 cup chopped mint
salt and pepper to taste
bed of lettuce leaves for serving
black olives, lemon wedges and tomato
   wedges to garnish

A little of this goes a long way as a starter to a meal. This is a super way of using fresh herbs from the garden.

Spread the bulgar out over a clean muslin cloth. (A clean tea-towel will be all right.) Sprinkle the bulgar with water and leave to rest for 30 minutes. Squeeze out the excess water. Mix in the onion, oil, lemon juice, herbs, salt and pepper. If you prefer it a little spicy, add a pinch of either cayenne pepper or ground cumin. Arrange the lettuce leaves on a large serving dish. Pile the bulgar wheat on top and garnish with the olives, lemon and tomato wedges.

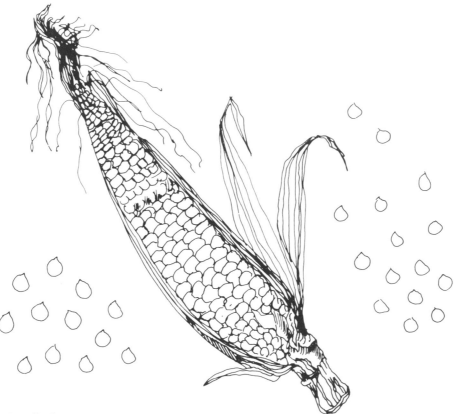

Corn on the Cob

Remove the husks, silk and any under-developed corn from the cobs, then put them into a pan of boiling water. Do not add salt to the water, as it tends to harden the corn. Boil uncovered in the pan for about 10 minutes or until the corn is tender. Drain well, and serve with salt and butter.

1 cob per person (as a starter)
butter to serve, margarine if preferred

Cheese and Nut Roast

Serve this roast with new potatoes and runner beans fresh from the garden.
   Grease a 9 inch (23 cm) baking tin. In a bowl, mix all the ingredients together. Check the seasoning and pour the mixture into the baking tin. Bake for 45 minutes at 350°F / 180°C / Mark 5. Serve the roast hot or cold.

2 oz / 60 g / ½ cup ground hazelnuts
2 oz / 60 g / ½ cup ground Brazil nuts
4 oz / 125 g / 1 cup roasted peanuts
   (unsalted)
2 oz / 60 g / ¼ cup margarine
2 eggs, beaten
4 oz / 125 g / 2 cups wholemeal breadcrumbs
6 oz / 175 g / 1½ cups grated Cheddar
   cheese
1 tsp sage
pinch cayenne pepper

Pasta and Lentil Bake

12 oz / 375 g / 3 cups cooked pasta shapes
4 oz / 125 g / 1½ cups cooked red lentils
3 tbsp oil
2 onions, finely chopped
1 clove garlic, crushed
1½ lb / 750 g / 6 cups fresh sliced tomatoes
8 oz / 250 g / 4 cups sliced mushrooms
½ tsp dried oregano
¼ tsp ground mace
5 fl oz / 140 ml / 1 cup tomato purée
salt and pepper

Sauce
1 oz / 25 g / 2 tbsp butter or margarine
1 oz / 25 g / 4 tbsp plain flour
¾ pint / 450 ml / 2 cups milk
pinch dry mustard powder
2 eggs, beaten

Topping
4 oz / 125 g / 1 cup grated Cheddar cheese
few pats of margarine

Cook the pasta in boiling salted water for 10 minutes. Heat the oil in a pan, and sauté the onion and garlic for a few minutes. Add the tomatoes and mushrooms, and cook until soft. Add the herbs, seasoning and tomato purée .

To make the sauce, first melt the butter. Add the flour, and cook for 2 minutes. Gradually add the milk. Season and add the mustard powder. Allow to cool slightly before beating in the eggs. Put a layer of the vegetables in the bottom of an ovenproof baking dish. Top with a layer of lentils, then pasta, then sauce. Repeat, ending with the sauce layer. Sprinkle over the cheese. Dot with the margarine. Bake for 25 minutes until golden brown at 350°F / 180°C / Mark 4.

Curried Vegetable Flan

Set the oven to 375°F / 190°C / Mark 5. For the flan case, mix the fat into the flour. Add enough cold water – about 4 tbsp – to make a smooth pliable dough. Line a 9 inch (22 cm) flan tin with the pastry and bake blind for 10 minutes. Remove the baking beans and bake for a further 5 minutes.

For the filling, heat a little oil in a pan. Add all the vegetables except the beans and peas. Cook for 5 minutes over a low heat. Stir in the curry powder and cook for another 5 minutes. Stir in the milk, beans and peas. Cook for 2 minutes. Stir in the cream, egg yolks and cheese. Cook for 1 minute. Pour into the flan case and bake for 25–30 minutes. Serve immediately.

Flan case
8 oz / 250 g / 2 cups plain wholemeal flour
5 oz / 150 g / ⅝ cup margarine

Filling
1 onion, finely chopped
1 clove garlic, crushed
2 sticks celery
1 large carrot, chopped
4oz / 125 g / 1 cup chopped runner beans
2 oz / 50 g / ½ cup fresh shelled peas
1 tsp curry powder
¼ pint / 150 ml / ⅔ cup milk
¼ pint / 150 ml / ⅔ cup single cream
3 egg yolks
2 oz / 50 g / ½ cup grated Cheddar Cheese

Tuscan Salad

Put the breadcrumbs into a bowl and mix in the oil and vinegar. Mix thoroughly until the crumbs begin to stick together. Deseed the green pepper and chop it very finely. Chop the tomatoes, and dice the cucumber. Add these to the crumbs, with the garlic and seasoning. Chill before serving, garnished with the tarragon.

12 oz / 375 g / 6 cups wholemeal breadcrumbs (1-day-old bread)
¼ pint / 150 ml / ⅔ cup cold pressed olive oil
3 tbsp red wine vinegar
1 small green pepper
4 tomatoes
½ cucumber
2 cloves garlic, crushed
salt and pepper to taste
1 tsp fresh chopped tarragon

Soya Mayonnaise

½ pint / 300 ml / 1⅓ cups soya milk,
   sweetened or unsweetened, as preferred
¼ pint / 150 ml / ⅔ cup olive or sunflower
   oil
salt and pepper to taste
pinch of paprika
3 tsp lemon juice

This is especially for people who are on gluten free, low fat or vegan diets.

Pour the soya milk into a blender. Add the oil, a few drops at a time to prevent curdling. Season to taste, and add the paprika. Lastly, add the lemon juice. Store in a bottle or jar in the refrigerator.

Tofu and Mushroom Salad with Sweet and Sour Dressing

6 oz / 175 g / 1⅙ cups diced fresh tofu
¼ lb / 125 g / 2 cups thinly sliced
   mushrooms
1¼ lb / 625 g / 4 cups fresh cooked sweetcorn kernels
1 stick celery, diced
2 medium tomatoes, diced
salt and pepper to taste

Dressing
juice of 2 limes
2 tbsp honey
8 tbsp sunflower oil
1 tsp paprika
¼ tsp onion salt
1 clove garlic, crushed
½ tsp celery seed
¼ tsp dry English mustard
ground black pepper

Toss all the salad ingredients together in a serving bowl. Put the ingredients for the dressing into a large screw-top jar, and shake vigorously to mix. Pour the dressing over the salad and serve.

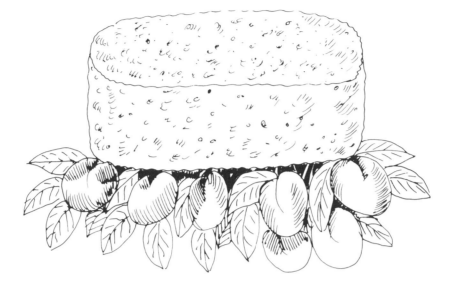

Upside Down Plum Cake

Cook the plums and drain them, reserving the juice for a sauce. Grease a 7 inch (18 cm) round cake tin. Cream the butter and sugar together and spread it over the bottom of the tin. Arrange the plums on top of this.

For the cake, cream the margarine and sugar together until light and fluffy. Add the beaten egg a little at a time and beat well, adding a little flour to prevent curdling. Fold in the remaining flour. Add the milk to give the batter a soft dropping consistency. Pour the mixture over the plums, spread it level and bake for about 45 minutes at 350°F / 180°C / Mark 4 until golden brown. Make a sauce with the reserved plum juice thickened with arrowroot and sweetened with a little sugar if desired.

Topping
1 lb / 500 g / 3 cups plums
2 oz / 60 g / ¼ cup butter
2 oz / 60 g / ⅓ cup light Muscovado sugar

Cake
4 oz / 125 g / ⅔ cup light Muscovado sugar
4 oz / 125 g / ½ cup vegetable margarine
2 beaten eggs
6 oz / 175 g / 1½ cups self-raising flour
2 tbsp milk

Peanut Crispies

Grease a baking sheet really well. Beat the egg whites until frothy. Gradually beat in the sugar, and continue beating until the mixture is stiff. Fold in the peanuts and vanilla extract. Drop heaped teaspoonfuls of the mixture on to the baking sheet, leaving room in between for them to spread. Bake for 15–20 minutes at 350°F / 180°C / Mark 4. Let them cool before removing them from the baking sheet.

3 egg whites
3 oz / 90 g / ½ cup light Muscovado sugar
6 oz / 200 g / 1½ cups ground peanuts
drop of vanilla extract

Blackberry and Apple Cake

4 oz / 125 g / ½ cup soft margarine
6 oz / 175 g / 1 cup light Muscovado sugar
2 eggs
6 oz / 175 g / 1½ cups plain flour
½ tsp almond extract
2 oz / 60 g / ½ cup ground almonds
1 tsp baking powder
1 lb / 500 g / 3 cups cooking apples
4 oz / 125 g / 1 cup blackberries
1 oz / 60 g / ¼ cup flaked almonds

Beat the margarine and sugar until light and fluffy. Beat in the eggs and a little flour to prevent curdling. Beat in the almond extract and ground almonds. Fold in the remaining flour with the baking powder. Core and slice the apples.

Spread two-thirds of the cake mixture in a greased and lined 8 inch (20 cm) cake tin. Layer the apple over the cake mixture. Stir the blackberries into the remaining cake mixture. Spread this over the apples. Sprinkle the flaked almonds over the top. Bake for 30 minutes at 375°F / 190°C / Mark 5. Turn the heat down to 350°F / 180°C / Mark 4 for a further 30 minutes, until cooked.

Baked Pears

6 large Comice or William pears
¼ pint / 150 ml / ⅔ cup water
6 oz / 175 g / 1 cup medium Muscovado
  sugar
4 whole cloves
½ cinnamon stick
juice of 1 lemon
4 oz / 125 g / 1 cup fine shred marmalade

Peel, core and halve the pears and place them in a buttered baking dish. Combine the water, sugar and spices in a saucepan, and heat until the sugar dissolves. Stir in the lemon juice and marmalade. Pour this over the pears. Bake for 20 minutes at 350°F / 180°C / Mark 4, basting occasionally.

Rowan and Apple Jelly

2 lb / 1 kg / 8 cups rowan berries

2 lb / 1 kg / 6½ cups crab apples (Bramleys will suffice)

juice of 2 lemons

½ tsp ground cloves

1 lb / 500 g / 2⅔ cups Demerara sugar for each pint / 625 ml / 2½ cups of liquid

*For this recipe you will need a **jelly bag**, which is a special cloth bag made from fine cotton. Alternatively, you can use a double thickness of fine white cotton. Attach the four corners firmly to something like an upturned stool. Put a bowl underneath to catch the liquid. Pour the fruit into the cloth and allow it to drip through. Do not try to assist it as the resulting jelly will be cloudy.*

Wash the berries and apples thoroughly. Put them into a large pan with the lemon juice and cloves, and pour on enough water to just cover. Bring to the boil, and simmer for 1 hour. Pour the fruit into a jelly bag, and leave it to hang overnight. Measure the liquid and return to the pan. Add 1 lb / 500 g / 2⅔ cups Demerara sugar to every pint / 625 ml / 2½ cups of liquid. Dissolve the sugar and then bring to the boil until setting point is reached. Pour into warm jars (page 16), then label and cover them.

Indian Chutney

1½ lb / 750 g / 5 cups chopped cooking apples

8 oz / 250 g / 1½ cups chopped fresh peaches

8 oz / 250 g / 1½ cups chopped fresh apricots

2 oz / 60 g / ⅓ cup sultanas

about 14 fl oz / 310 ml / 1¼ cups white wine vinegar

6 cloves garlic, crushed

2 inch (5 cm) piece fresh root ginger, peeled and grated

14 oz / 425 g / 2⅓ cups light Muscovado sugar

2 tsp salt

½ tsp cayenne pepper

Put all the fruit into a large pan. Pour on enough of the vinegar to just cover. Simmer for about half an hour, until soft. Add the remaining ingredients and simmer gently until the mixture is thick and soft. Bottle into clean jars (page 16). Store the chutney in a cool, dry, dark place.

Runner Bean Chutney

Cook the beans in boiling salted water until tender. Strain them into a large pan, add the vinegar (reserving a little to mix the spices in) and onion, and cook for 10 minutes. Mix the spices and reserved vinegar to a paste in another bowl. Add this to the beans, with the sugar, bring to the boil and simmer until thick – about 30 minutes. Bottle the chutney in clean jars while still hot (page 16). Store in a cool, dry place.

2 lb / 1 kg / 6 cups runner beans, trimmed and sliced
1½ pints / 925 ml / 3¾ cups cider vinegar
1½ lb / 750 g / 6 cups finely chopped onion
1 level tbsp turmeric
1 heaped tbsp English mustard powder
1 lb / 500 g / 2⅔ cups light Muscovado sugar
1 lb / 500 g / 2⅔ cups Demerara sugar

Plum Sauce

This is a good, tangy sauce to serve with vegetables, or nut or lentil cutlets.

Put all the ingredients into a large pan. Bring to the boil, and then simmer for 1–1½ hours until it is thick and there is no liquid left on the surface. If you like a really smooth sauce, you can pass it through a food processor or Mouli Mill. Pour the sauce into clean jars or bottles while still hot. Label them and cover tightly. Store in a cool, dry place.

2½ lb / 1¼ kg / 8 cups stoned plums
1 lb / 500 g / 4 cups peeled chopped onions
¼ pint / 150 ml / ⅔ cup cider vinegar
2 tsp salt
1 tsp ground ginger
1 tsp ground allspice
1 tsp ground nutmeg
1 tsp dried English mustard
¼ tsp ground cloves
4 oz / 125 g / ⅔ cup medium Muscovado sugar

OCTOBER

Summer is well and truly over now, and it's time for some cheering autumnal food. Try Baked Potato Skins with Chili Bean Filling (page 123) if you feel you need warming up!

There are still plenty of hedgerow fruits around. Go out on a gathering expedition and make some delicious Hedgerow Jam (page 128). Pears and apples are plentiful – make the most of them with Cider Apple Cake, Apple Charlotte and Pear and Blackberry Tart. As Winter approaches we can justify eating slightly heavier puddings.

If you can get hold of elderberries, you can make a delicious fruit sauce (page 126) to bottle and have on hand to brighten up nut rissoles or cutlets. Preserve-making continues, with chutneys and pickled onions (page 125).

With the weather getting chillier and the days getting shorter, the produce in the garden grows less. The hardier varieties of Winter vegetables are now available – leeks, parsnips, spinach, cabbage and celery. Harvest root vegetables from your garden and store them. This month will see the end of the runner beans.

The fields on a nice humid day should still be full of wild mushrooms. They have a marvellous flavour, so it is a good idea to prepare a few dishes based on mushrooms for freezing. Mushrooms in Cider, Mushroom Pâté and Mushroom Soup make luxurious starters; Barley and Mushroom Casserole (page 124) is very filling and freezes well.

Hallowe'en is at the end of the month. Try to have a couple of pumpkins growing in the garden, even if you only want to make lanterns out of them – they are so easy to grow. Traditionally, turnip or pumpkin lanterns were hung outside the house to frighten all the ghoulies and ghosties that were supposed to be abroad on this night; nowadays they're more often used to scare the neighbours!

Cream of Pumpkin Soup

2 lb / 1 kg / 7 cups prepared weight of
    pumpkin
2 small onions, finely chopped
2 oz / 60 g / ¼ cup butter or margarine
2 oz / 60 g / ½ cup flour
1 pint / 625 ml / 2½ cups milk
salt and pepper
1 pint / 625 ml / 2½ cups vegetable stock
2 oz / 60 g / ½ cup grated Cheddar cheese
¼ pint / 150 ml / 1 cup single cream
parsley to garnish

This is a good way of using up the scooped out flesh from your pumpkin lantern.

Fry the pumpkin and onion in the melted butter gently for 5 minutes. Stir in the flour. Gradually stir in the milk and seasoning. Add the stock, and continue to simmer for 5 minutes. Put the soup through a sieve or blender, then return it to the pan. Stir in the cheese and cream. Add the parsley to the bowls when you are serving the soup.

Mushroom Soup

8 oz / 250 g / 4 cups finely chopped
    mushrooms
1 onion, finely chopped
2 oz / 60 g / ¼ cup butter or margarine
1½ oz / 50 g / 6 tbsp flour
1 pint / 625 ml / 2½ cups milk
salt and pepper
pinch ground mace
1½ pints / 930 ml / 3¾ cups vegetable stock

Melt the butter in a large saucepan and add the mushrooms and onion. Cook for 1 minute. Stir in the flour, and cook gently for 3 minutes. Add the milk gradually, stirring all the time. Season well and add the mace. Stir in the stock. Bring to the boil, reduce to a simmer, and cook for 5 minutes. Remove a couple of spoonfuls of the mushrooms to add to the soup later. Run the remaining soup through a blender. Stir in the mushrooms. Add the cream and slowly reheat. Serve immediately.

Mushroom Pâté

Drain the peas, pour on fresh water, and cook. They should take about 40 minutes. Heat a little oil in a pan, and fry the celery, onions and garlic until light golden brown. Add the mushrooms, and cook for another 5 minutes. Mash the cooked peas with the tomato purée and other ingredients. Stir in the mushrooms and onion. Mix until smooth. Spoon into ramekin dishes and chill, before serving with melba toast.

6 oz / 185 g / 1 cup blackeyed peas, soaked overnight
2 sticks celery
1 medium onion, finely chopped
2 cloves garlic, crushed
6 oz / 185 g / 3 cups mushrooms, chopped
2 tsp tomato purée
1 tsp vegetable extract
1 tbsp fresh chopped parsley
4 oz / 125 g / ½ cup finely chopped black olives
2 tbsp sherry

Mushrooms in Cider

Wipe the mushrooms and slice them thickly. Heat the oil in a pan. Add the onion, and cook until light golden brown. Add the mushrooms, herbs and cider. Season, cover and simmer very gently for 15 minutes. Serve with crusty bread.

1 lb / 500 g / 8 cups mushrooms
2 tbsp olive oil
1 onion, finely chopped
pinch oregano
1 tbsp finely chopped fresh parsley
¼ pint / 150 ml / 1 cup sweet cider
salt and pepper to taste

Leeks and Celery Au Gratin

3 leeks, trimmed, washed and shredded
4 large sticks celery
salt and pepper
2 oz / 60 g / ¼ cup butter
2 oz / 60 g / ½ cup flour
1 tsp mustard powder
¼ tsp turmeric
½ pint / 300 ml / 1⅓ cups milk
6 oz / 185 g / 1½ cups grated Cheddar
   cheese
3 tbsp breadcrumbs

Sauté the leeks and celery in a little oil for 5 minutes. Add ¼ pint / 150 ml / ⅔ cup water. Season, cover, and cook until the vegetables are tender. Put them into an oven-proof baking dish. In another pan, melt the butter. Stir in the flour, mustard powder and turmeric, and cook for 2 minutes. Gradually add the milk, stirring all the time to make a smooth sauce. Pour the sauce over the leeks and celery. Mix the cheese and breadcrumbs together and sprinkle them over the top. Brown in the oven at 375°F / 190°C / Mark 5 for 15 minutes.

Bubble and Squeak

1 lb / 500 g / 3 cups mashed but fairly firm
   potato
1 lb / 500 g / 3 cups cooked cabbage (the
   white variety is really nice)
a little cooked onion or leek (this adds a bit
   more flavour)
salt and pepper

Traditionally this incorporated bacon, but as this is a vegetarian book, we have dispensed with that. But this is still a good way of using up leftover cooked potatoes and cabbage. You can, of course, use whatever leftover vegetables you fancy.

    Heat some butter or oil in a large frying pan. Mix the vegetables together well and season them. Press the vegetables into the pan. Fry gently until the bottom is golden brown. Turn and cook the other side. Serve immediately.

Cheese Fondue

This is simple to make and a surprisingly filling meal.

Rub the garlic around the inside of a heavy based saucepan or cheese fondue pot. Pour in the wine and lemon juice. Heat through gently. Gradually add the cheese a little at a time, stirring constantly to aid the melting process. Mix the Kirsch in a little bowl with the flour, cayenne pepper, black pepper and nutmeg. Stir into the cheese and cook until thick. If the fondue becomes too thick before serving, add a little more wine. Serve with cubes of wholemeal or French bread and slices of raw vegetables such as carrots, apples, onions and tomatoes.

1 large clove garlic
1 pint / 625 ml / 2½ cups dry white wine
2 tsp lemon juice
¾ lb / 375 g / 3 cups Gruyère cheese, grated
¾ lb / 375 g / 3 cups Emmenthal cheese, grated (you could substitute Edam for one of these cheeses)
3 tbsp Kirsch
3 tbsp wholemeal flour
pinch cayenne pepper
freshly ground black pepper
grated nutmeg

Baked Potato Skins with Chili Bean Filling

Cut the potatoes in half lengthwise. Scoop out most of the potato flesh (use for soup?) leaving a thickness of about ¼ inch (5 cm) all around. Place on a greased baking sheet and bake for about 45 minutes until crisp at 375°F / 190°C / Mark 6.

For the filling, heat a little oil in a saucepan. Gently fry the onion and garlic until soft. Add the peppers and cook for 3 minutes to soften slightly. Stir in the spices and cook for 3 minutes. Add the tomatoes, purée and kidney beans. Simmer very gently for 45 minutes in a covered pan. Spoon into the crisply baked potatoes and serve with a fresh green salad.

6 large well-scrubbed old potatoes
8 oz / 250 g / 1⅓ cups cooked red kidney beans
2 medium onions, finely chopped
2 cloves garlic, finely chopped
1 medium green pepper, deseeded and chopped
1 heaped tsp chili powder
1 level tsp paprika
½ tsp ground cumin
ground pepper and salt
14 oz / 400 ml / 2 cups canned tomatoes
3 tbsp tomato purée

Soya and Sunflower Burgers

6 oz / 185 g / 1 cup soya beans
3 oz / 90 g / ¾ cup sunflower seeds (grind 2
   oz / 60 g / ½ cup of them)
1 medium onion, finely chopped
1 small green pepper, finely chopped
2 tsp soya sauce
2 tbsp fresh chopped parsley
salt and pepper to taste
egg to bind and coat the burgers (unless you
   wish to keep them vegan in which case
   you can use a little soya milk)
soya bran or wholemeal breadcrumbs to
   coat

Soak the soya beans overnight, then drain off the water and pour on fresh. Cook for 3–4 hours until they are soft enough to mash. Heat a little oil in a pan and gently fry the onion and green pepper. Put the soya beans into a bowl and mash them, stir in the ground sunflower seeds and the whole ones, the seasoning, and the vegetables. Stir in the required amount of milk or egg. Shape into 6 burgers, brush with egg or soya milk, roll in soya bran or breadcrumbs and then fry until light golden brown. You can, if you prefer, bake the burgers for 20 minutes at 350°F / 180°C / Mark 4. Serve hot or cold.

Barley and Mushroom Casserole

3 large onions, sliced
12 oz / 375 g / 6 cups sliced mushrooms
2 green peppers, finely chopped
12 oz / 375 g / 2 cups pot barley, soaked
   overnight in cold water
⅓ pint / 210 ml / 1 cup water and 1 heaped
   tsp vegetable extract
1 lb 14 oz / 900 g / 4½ cups canned tomatoes
1 tsp dried thyme
2 tbsp chopped fresh parsley

Heat a little oil in a pan. Fry the onions until light golden brown. Add the mushrooms and peppers, and cook for 2 minutes. Put the barley in a casserole dish. Add the water, vegetable extract and tomatoes. Stir in the cooked vegetables and herbs. Cover and bake at 350°F / 180°C / Mark 4 for 1 hour, until the barley is tender.

Stuffed Marrow

Pre-cook the brown rice and buckwheat in boiling salted water for about 40 minutes. Fry the onion and garlic in a little oil. Stir in the cooked buckwheat and rice. Mix in the marjoram, cayenne, seasoning, cheese, hazelnuts, tomatoes and tomato purée. Wash the marrow and cut it in half. Scoop out the seeds. Spoon the rice mixture into the marrow halves and place one half on top of the other. Wrap in tin foil or greased wax paper and place in an ovenproof dish. Bake the stuffed marrow for 1 hour at 350°F / 180°C / Mark 4.

8 oz / 250 g / 2 cups brown rice
4 oz / 125 g / ⅔ cup roasted buckwheat
1 medium onion
2 cloves garlic
1 tbsp marjoram
¼ tsp cayenne
salt and pepper to season
10 oz / 310 g / 2½ cups Cheddar cheese
4 oz / 125 g / 1 cup chopped hazelnuts
1 lb / 500 g / 4 cups chopped tomatoes
3 tbsp tomato purée
2 lb / 1 kg / 1 large marrow

Spiced Vinegar

Put all the ingredients in a bowl, and stand it in a saucepan of water. Bring the water to the boil, and then take the pan off the heat and allow to stand a couple of hours. Strain and bottle.

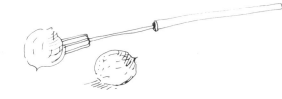

2 pints / 1¼ litres / 5 cups cider vinegar
1 x 5 inch (13 cm) piece cinnamon bark
1 tsp whole cloves
1 tsp whole allspice
1 tsp blade mace
a few black peppercorns
3 dried chillies
1 x 2 inch (5 cm) piece root ginger, bruised

Pickled Onions

Pour the water into a large bowl and mix in the sea salt. Drop in the onions still in their skins, and leave them to soak overnight. Drain the onions, and then pour boiling water over them to loosen the skins. Peel them, then transfer them to another bowl. Sprinkle again with salt, and leave overnight. In the morning, rinse the onions well under cold water. Dry them thoroughly, and put into clean, large jars. Pour the vinegar over to top the onions. Label and seal with rustproof lids. Store for at least 6 weeks before using.

5 pints / 3 litres / 3 quarts water
1 lb / 500 g / 2 cups fine sea salt
4 lb / 2 kg / 10 cups pickling onions
1½ pints / 925 ml / 4 cups spiced cider vinegar

Marrow Chutney

3 lb / 1½ kg / 10 cups vegetable marrow,
    peeled and cubed
salt
2 medium apples, cored and minced
2 medium onions, peeled and minced
1½ pints / 925 ml / 3¼ cups cider vinegar
4 oz / 125 g / ⅔ cup medium Muscovado
    sugar
8 oz / 250 g / 1¼ cups sultanas
12 peppercorns
2 inch (5 cm) piece root ginger, bruised
¼ tsp garam masala

Put the marrow in a large bowl and sprinkle it with salt. Leave overnight, then drain, rinse and dry it. Put it into a large pan with the apples, onions, vinegar, sugar and sultanas. Tie the peppercorns and ginger in a piece of muslin, attach this to the saucepan handle and lower into the chutney. Sprinkle the garam masala into the pan. Bring to the boil, stirring continuously until the sugar dissolves. Reduce to a simmer, and cook until thick and brown – about an hour. Remove the spices, then bottle the chutney (page 16).

Elderberry Sauce

2 lb / 1 kg / 8 cups ripe elderberries
¾ pint / 450 ml / 2 cups water
pinch salt
12 whole cloves
4 whole black peppercorns
4 finely chopped shallots
pinch ground mace

This sauce is ideal to serve with savoury rissoles or cutlets.

Put the elderberries stripped from their stalks into an ovenproof dish, and cook overnight in a very slow oven. Strain them through a sieve, put them in a pan with the other ingredients and bring to the boil. Reduce to a simmer for 20 minutes until thick. Bottle when cold (page 16), including the spices.

Apple Charlotte

Cook the apples, lemon and spices until tender. Spread the bread with the margarine and arrange around the sides and bottom of an 8 inch (20 cm) baking dish. Mix the sultanas into the apples and pour onto the bread in the baking dish. Mix the sugar and breadcrumbs together. Sprinkle over the apples and bake for 45 minutes at 350°F / 180°C / Mark 4.

1 lb / 500 g / 3 cups cooking apples, sliced, cored and chopped
rind and juice of ½ lemon
½ level tsp ground cinnamon
pinch ground cloves
6 thin slices wholemeal bread
2 oz / 60 g / ¼ cup vegetable margarine
3 oz / 90 g / ½ cup sultanas
3 oz / 90 g / ½ cup Muscovado sugar
3 tbsp wholemeal breadcrumbs

Pear and Blackberry Tart

Rub the margarine into the flour. Add about 3 or 4 tbsp water, enough to make a pliable dough. Roll out the pastry and line a 9 inch (22 cm) flan tin. Bake the pastry blind for 20 minutes at 375°F / 190°C / Mark 5.

Prepare the filling by making a syrup with the sugar and water in a saucepan. Heat until the sugar dissolves. Slice the pears and cook them in the syrup until just tender. Drain the pears, reserving some of the syrup to make a sauce – you will need ¼ pint / 150 ml / ⅔ cup. Gently stew the blackberries in a separate pan until they are just cooked. Reserve 8 pear slices for the top of the flan. Pulp the remaining pears, and stir in the egg yolk and lemon juice. Lay the blackberries on top of the pears. Mix the arrowroot with a little of the syrup, add the rest of the syrup, and heat until thick. Spread this sauce over the fruit. Decorate with the pear halves.

6 oz / 180 g / 1½ cups wholemeal flour
3 oz / 90 g / 1¾ cups vegetable margarine

Filling
8 oz / 250 g / 1⅓ cups Demerara sugar and ¾ pint / 450 ml / 2 cups water
4 large ripe pears, peeled and cored
½ lb / 250 g / 2 cups blackberries
2 tsp arrowroot
1 egg yolk
juice of 1 lemon

Cider Apple Cake

1 lb / 500 g / 4 cups wholemeal self-raising
    flour
4 oz / 125 g / medium Muscovado sugar
6 oz / 185 g / ¾ cup vegetable margarine
1 tbsp molasses
1 tbsp malt extract
2 medium eggs
¼ pint / 150 ml / ⅔ cup sweet cider

Topping
1½ oz / 45 g / ⅓ cup chopped walnuts
3 tbsp vegetable margarine
1½ oz / 45 g / ⅜ cup wholemeal flour
1 lb / 500 g / 3 cups chopped Cox's apples
2 oz / 60 g / ⅓ cup Demerara sugar
½ tsp ground cinnamon

Beat all the cake ingredients together. Pour into a greased and lined 8 inch (20 cm) round cake tin. Mix the topping ingredients together in a bowl then sprinkle over the top of the cake. Bake the cake at 350°F / 180°C / Mark 4 for 1–1¼ hours.

Hedgerow Jam

1 lb / 500 g / 4 cups elderberries
1 lb / 500 g / 3 cups blackberries
¾ lb / 375 g / 3 cups rosehips
½ lb / 250 g / 2 cups haws
¾ lb / 375 g / 3 cups rowan berries
½ lb / 250 g / 2 cups sloes
1 pint / 625 ml / 2½ cups water
1 lb / 500 g / 3 cups cooking apples, crab
    apples or windfalls
6 lb / 3 kg / 16 cups Demerara sugar

Strip the elderberries from their stalks using a fork for ease. Put them into a large pan with the other berries and the water. Cook very gently until tender – about 1 hour. Put the roughly chopped apples into another large pan, and strain in the elderberry mixture. Bring to the boil, then simmer until cooked. Add the sugar, and heat slowly to dissolve. Bring to the boil, and continue to boil until setting point is reached. Test for setting and bottle (page 16).

Blackberry Gin

2½ lb / 1.25 kg / 8 cups ripe blackberries
9 oz / 300 g / 1½ cups Demerara sugar
1¾ pints / 1 litre / 6½ cups gin

Make it this month ready for Christmas treats.

Crush the fruit lightly and put into a large jar. Stir in the sugar. Pour the gin over the top and seal the jar tightly. Give it a daily shake for one month. Leave to stand for about another 2 months. Filter into sterilised bottles and cork.

Rosehip Syrup

This is a great source of vitamin C. Two teaspoons daily will help protect you against colds and 'flu.

Wash and mince the rosehips. Bring the water to the boil in a large pan; add the rosehips. Bring back to the boil and then simmer for 45 minutes. Allow to cool, then sieve through a jelly bag (see page 87). Leave overnight to strain to make sure all the juice has run through. Return the juice to the pan and then reduce by half in volume by simmering gently. Add the sugar, and simmer gently until dissolved. Bring to the boil, and boil for a further 5 minutes. Pour into clean warm bottles. Cork the bottles tightly and label them. As it does not keep more than a couple of weeks once opened, it is best to use small bottles.

2 lb / 1 kg / 8 cups ripe rosehips
4½ pints / 2.8 litres / 11¼ cups water
1 lb / 500 g / 2⅔ cups Demerara sugar

Ginger Beer

This is another of my Grandmother's recipes which brings back happy childhood memories. It is very thirst quenching and can also help settle upset stomachs.

Dissolve 1 tsp sugar in a little of the warm water. Stir in the yeast, and leave to activate for 15 minutes. Add the rest of the water and 1 tsp ground ginger. Put into a large jar and cover with a piece of muslin. Then, every day for a week add 1 tsp each of ginger and sugar.

Dissolve the Demerara sugar in the boiling water. Add the lemon juice, cold water and the starter. Bottle and cork – but not too tightly – and leave to ferment. Ginger beer can be drunk after the third day.

Starter
8 tsp sugar
¾ pint / 450 ml / 2 cups warm water
½ tsp fresh yeast
8 tsp ground ginger

12 oz / 375 g / 2 cups Demerara sugar
1 pint / 625 ml / 2⅓ cups boiling water
juice of 1 lemon
2½ pints / 1½ litres / 6 cups cold water

NOVEMBER

November in England brings the anniversary of the unsuccessful Gunpowder Plot to blow up the Houses of Parliament. America has Thanksgiving Day, dating back to the settlement of the first pioneers. It was a celebration of the survival of a winter and having gone on to produce a harvest the following year. Generally, a turkey is featured as a meal, but vegetarians can try the Chestnut and Peanut Christmas Roast (page 146).

Whether you celebrate Guy Fawkes' Night with fireworks or not, it's a good time to have a bonfire to clear up the garden. Always check before lighting it in case hedgehogs have crawled in to hibernate. It is possible to cook jacket potatoes in the bottom of the fire, providing you have managed to build one that burns slowly and does not disappear at the strike of a match! Wrap the scrubbed potatoes in tin foil and then bury them in the base of the fire – make sure you remember where you put them. This method takes a lot longer than cooking them in a domestic oven so start them off at least two hours before you need them. While they are cooking, you can carry on with the gardening – this is the time to plant rhubarb, Jerusalem artichokes and horseradish and sow broad beans and peas.

Christmas is drawing nearer, so it is time to start doing some preparation. Christmas cake and pudding taste better if they are made a month beforehand. The family will doubtless enjoy helping to mix the puddings and cakes – and scraping the bowls afterwards.

Store your Christmas cake in an airtight tin and leave decorating it until just before Christmas day itself. You can cover it with marzipan (recipe, page 45) and if you feel that no Christmas cake is complete without its layer of royal icing, go ahead – it's only once a year! Alternatively, stud it with glacé fruits and nuts for a really festive appearance.

Porridge

Cold mornings call for a hot breakfast! This is an old-fashioned method of making porridge. Oatmeal is still used widely today but it is so economical and nourishing that it is a wonder it is not more popular. It is a lot cheaper than your average breakfast cereal and certainly more nutritious. And there are currently reports that oatmeal can help in reducing cholesterol levels in the blood.

Using 1 oz / 25 g / ⅛ cup of oatmeal per person, leave the oatmeal to soak overnight in 6 fl oz / 170 ml / 1 cup of water or milk or a mixture of the two. In the morning, cook gently for 5 or 6 minutes. Add a pinch of salt if desired. Serve as it is, or with milk and some unrefined sugar or honey.

Watercress Soup

2 large bunches of watercress
1 shallot or small onion
2 peeled potatoes
2 pints / 1¼ litres / 5 cups mild-flavoured
   vegetable stock
pinch nutmeg
plenty of freshly ground pepper
salt to taste
5 fl oz / 150 ml / 1 cup cream

My mother's old faithful recipe, and one of our family favourites.

Finely dice the onion. Roughly chop the potatoes, and chop the watercress, discarding the tougher pieces of stalk. Reserve a few leaves whole for the garnish. Gently cook the vegetables in a little oil or butter in a covered pan. Stir them occasionally to prevent sticking. Add the stock, nutmeg and seasoning and slowly bring to the boil. Reduce the heat, and continue to simmer until the vegetables are soft. Allow to cool slightly, and then put the soup through a blender so it is roughly chopped. Reheat and stir in the cream, but do not boil. Serve, garnished with the reserved leaves.

French Onion Soup

4 large onions, thickly sliced
2 cloves garlic
1 tsp sugar
2 pints / 1¼ litres / 5 cups vegetable stock
pinch mace, salt and pepper
4 oz / 125 g / 1 cup Cheddar or Gruyère
   cheese, thinly sliced
4 slices of toast or French bread

This is my very favourite soup, something I make gallons of to put in the deep freeze.

Cook the onions and garlic in a little oil and the sugar. Stir to prevent sticking. When they are golden brown, pour in the stock. Bring to the boil, and simmer for ½–¾ hour, covered. Season to taste. Serve in soup bowls, topped with a slice of toast each and the cheese on top of that. Put under the grill briefly to melt the cheese.

Bean and Brandy Pâté

Thoroughly mash the soya beans in a large bowl. Stir in the other ingredients, and pour into a greased and lined 2 lb / 1 kg loaf tin. Bake for 45–60 minutes at 375°F / 190°C / Mark 5 until firm. Allow the pâté to cool in the tin before turning it out.

8 oz / 250 g / 1⅓ cups cooked soya beans
5 fl oz / 150 ml / ⅔ cup soya milk
2 beaten eggs
2 tbsp brandy
2 tsp vegetable extract
2 tsp tamari
½ large onion, finely chopped
2 cloves garlic, crushed
½ tsp dried thyme
⅛ tsp ground allspice
⅛ tsp ground ginger
ground black pepper to taste

Potato, Leek and Cheese Bake

Preheat oven to 375°F / 190°C / Mark 5. Grease a 2 pint (1¼ litre) ovenproof dish. Peel and thinly slice the potatoes. Cut the leeks into ¾ inch (2 cm) pieces, and wash thoroughly. Layer the potatoes, leeks and cheese in the dish, seasoning to taste and finishing with a layer of cheese. Dab the margarine on the top. Dribble the milk over the top. Bake for 1¼ hours, until the potatoes are soft.

1½ lb / 750 g / 4 cups potatoes
1 lb / 500 g / 4 cups leeks
4 oz / 125 g / 1 cup grated Cheddar cheese
2 oz / 60 g / ¼ cup margarine
½ pt / 300 ml / 1½ cups milk
salt and pepper

Winter Vegetable Pie

Heat some oil in a pan and add all the vegetables except the tomatoes. Cook until transparent. Add the tomatoes, beans and vegetable extract. Add 1 tbsp plain flour and stir to thicken. Place in a 2 pint (1¼ litre) pie dish.

To make the pastry, grate the margarine into the flour. Break up with a knife. Add enough water to make a pliable dough then wrap it in a plastic bag. Chill for 10 minutes. Roll out a pie crust for the top. Egg glaze and bake for 30 to 35 minutes at 375°F / 190°C / Mark 5.

Filling
2 medium onions, peeled and sliced
2 medium carrots, scrubbed and chopped
2 sticks celery, chopped
8 oz / 250 g / 2 cups tomatoes, fresh or canned (if you use canned, omit the water in the recipe)
½ lb / 250 g / 1⅓ cups cooked butter or haricot beans (about ¼ lb / 125 g / ⅔ cup dry weight)
1 tsp vegetable extract
¼ pint / 150 ml / ⅔ cup water
1 tsp dried mixed herbs

Pastry
8 oz / 250 g / 2 cups plain wholemeal flour
6 oz / 180 g / ¾ cup margarine
cold water to mix

133

Bean and Spinach Pot

1 lb / 500 g / 2⅔ cups soya beans, soaked
  overnight

6 oz / 180 g / ¾ cup clarified butter or oil

1 large onion, chopped

6 cloves garlic, crushed

4 bay leaves

1 tsp cumin seeds

1 tsp turmeric powder

1 tsp chili powder

8 oz / 250 g / 2 cups fresh tomatoes

8 oz / 250 g / 4 cups spinach

1 inch (2.5 cm) piece fresh root ginger

1 tbsp garam masala

salt

Pre-cook the soya beans in boiling water until just tender – about 1 hour or so. Heat the butter or oil in a large pan. Fry the onion, garlic, bay leaves and cumin seed until the onion is golden brown. Add the beans, turmeric and chili powder, and stir well. Add the tomatoes and spinach. Add the ginger, garam masala, and salt to taste. Cook over a low heat for 15 minutes. When the butter or oil starts to separate, add about ¾ pint /450 ml / 2 cups of water. Now you can either leave the dish to gently simmer on the cooker for 1 hour or put it into a moderate oven. This is to let the flavour develop. Serve with rice or lentils.

Vegetable Curry

1 heaped tsp each of fenugreek seed, cumin
  seed, coriander seed, chili powder and
  turmeric

1 cinnamon stick

2 medium onions, chopped

2 cloves garlic, crushed

1 oz / 30 g / ⅛ cup crushed fresh ginger

2 oz / 60 g / ½ cup plain flour

14 oz / 400 g / 2 cups canned tomatoes, or
  use frozen

½ pint / 300 ml / 1⅓ cups water or vegetable
  stock

2 carrots, scrubbed and roughly chopped

3 potatoes, diced

½ small cauliflower in florets

1 parsnip, diced

1 large apple, chopped

½ small swede, chopped

Crush the spices using a pestle and mortar or rolling pin. Heat a little oil, and fry the spices for 3 minutes. Add the onion, garlic and ginger, and fry gently for 5 minutes. Stir in the flour, and cook lightly for a couple of minutes. Add tomatoes, stock and vegetables, and simmer gently for an hour. Serve on a bed of brown rice; it is also delicious in baked jacket potatoes.

Brown Rice

Allow 2 oz / 25 g / ¼ cup dry weight rice per person. Rinse the rice thoroughly to clean it. You will then need double the volume of boiling salted water to cook it in. Be sure your pan is big enough to allow for the rice to swell. Pour the rice into the water and then let it cook undisturbed until the rice has taken up all the water. This should be about 45 minutes – it may need a little longer. The rice should be light and fluffy. Cooking rice does vary in cooking times and personal preferences. Some people prefer it with a little bite to it.

Baked Red Cabbage

Grease a baking dish with half the margarine. Layer in the vegetables and apple, starting and finishing with the cabbage. Dot with the remaining margarine. Pour over the wine, water, sugar and seasoning. Cover tightly and bake for 2 hours at 300°F / 150°C / Mark 2.

3 tbsp margarine
1 small red cabbage, chopped
1 onion, peeled and chopped
2 cooking apples, grated
⅛ pint / 75 ml / ⅓ cup red wine (tee-totallers can use red wine vinegar)
⅛ pint / 75 ml / ⅓ cup water
2 tbsp raw sugar
salt and pepper

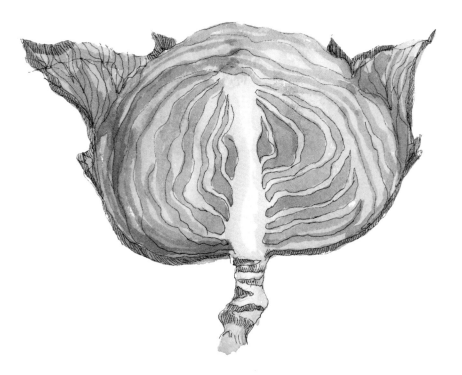

Autumn Lasagne

12 sheets of wholewheat lasagne
3 large potatoes, peeled and diced
1 large parsnip, peeled and chopped
3 large carrots, peeled and chopped
2 medium onions, finely chopped
14 oz / 375 g / 2 cups canned tomatoes
1 tbsp tomato purée
1½ tsp mixed herbs
salt and pepper to taste

Cheese Sauce
6 tbsp margarine
3 oz / 75 g / ¾ cup plain flour
½ tsp mustard powder
1 pint / 600 ml / 3 cups milk
8 oz / 225 g / 1 cup Cheddar cheese

Cook the lasagne in a large pan of boiling water; add a little oil to prevent the sheets sticking together. If you are using precooked lasagne continue on to the next step.

Put the potatoes, parsnip and carrots in a large pan of cold water, bring to the boil and cook for about 8 minutes or until they are slightly soft. Meanwhile, heat a little oil in a frying pan and cook the onions until soft. Drain the cooked vegetables and mix in the onions, tomatoes, tomatoe purée, herbs and salt and pepper.

Make the cheese sauce by melting the margarine and stirring in the flour and mustard powder. Cook for a couple of minutes. Gradually stir in the milk, mixing thoroughly to prevent it from becoming lumpy. When the sauce is smooth, stir in most of the cheese, reserving a little for the top. Using a deep dish, put a layer of the vegetables in the bottom, then a layer of lasagne, and then a little cheese sauce. Repeat, finishing with the cheese sauce. Sprinkle the remaining cheese on the top. Cook at 180°C / 350°F / Mark 4 for 30 minutes, or until nicely browned on top.

Jacket Potatoes

For a really substantial meal, which is inexpensive and full of goodness, what can beat jacket potatoes? They have well and truly placed themselves on the restaurant menu alongside the French Fries. Here we describe three routes to perfect baked potatoes, and give a selection of delicious fillings to put in them.

First, scrub the potatoes thoroughly and remove any undesirable bits. Prick them all over with a fork. They can then be cooked in several different ways:

Wrapped in foil and buried in the embers of a fire, they will take about two hours to cook, depending on the heat of the fire.

My favourite way of cooking them is directly in the oven; this way you get nice crispy skins. Scrub and prick the potatoes and arrange them on a baking tray. Place in a 190°C / 375°F / Mark 5 oven for about an hour. Squeeze them to see if they are soft. This is a good way to cook a lot of potatoes.

The third way to cook jacket potatoes is in the microwave. Here an average size potato will take about 8 minutes on high; multiply the time by the number of potatoes you are cooking. You can pop them in a hot oven afterwards for a few minutes to crisp them up.

For tasty fillings you can try some of the recipes in previous chapters:

Boston Baked Beans (page 32).
Chilli Bean Filling (page 123).
Leek and Celery Au Gratin (page 122).
Vegetable Curry (page 134).

Another couple of nice fillings are:

2 tablespoons of cooked sweetcorn added to 1 tablespoon of chopped cooked onion.

1 tablespoonful of low fat cheese mixed with
1 tablespoon of thick yogurt, a little crushed garlic
and a pinch of cayenne pepper.

Christmas Cake

1 tsp ground cinnamon

½ tsp ground nutmeg

½ tsp ground cloves

½ tsp salt

9 oz / 300 g / 2¼ cups wholemeal flour

4 oz / 125 g / ½ cup sultanas

4 oz / 125 g / ½ cup chopped soaked apricots

4 oz / 125 g / ½ cup glace cherries (optional)

10 oz / 310 g / 1¼ cups seeded raisins

4 oz / 125 g / ½ cup small raisins or currants

6 oz / 180 g / 1½ cups chopped unblanched almonds

8 oz / 250 g / 1 cup unsalted butter or margarine (butter gives the cake a better keeping quality)

1 lb / 500 g / 2⅔ cups medium Muscovado sugar or 6 dessertspoons honey plus 3 dessertspoons molasses

6 eggs, separated

1 tsp vanilla extract

4 fl oz / 125 ml / ⅔ cup brandy

Mix the spices and salt with ⅔ of the flour. Mix the dried fruit up with the remaining flour. Add the almonds to the fruit mixture. Cream the butter until soft. Mix in the sugar or honey, and continue to beat until creamy. Add the egg yolks and vanilla, and beat until fluffy. Add the flour mixture and brandy. Beat the egg whites until fluffy and fold them into the mixture. Pour into a greased and lined 9 inch (22 cm) round cake tin and bake in a 300°F / 150°C / Mark 2 oven for 1½ hours, then lower the temperature to 275°F / 140°C / Mark 1 for 2 hours.

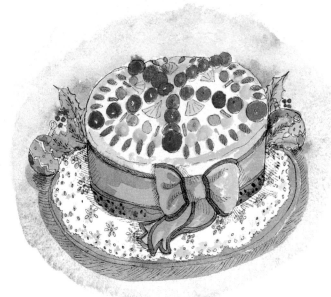

Christmas Pudding (Sugar Free)

This will make four one pint (600 ml) puddings.

Combine all the dried fruits together in a large mixing bowl. Add the peels, juices and brandy. Leave to stand overnight. Combine the flour, breadcrumbs, sugar, carrots, apples, spices, salt, and vegetable suet or butter with the fruit. It is easier if you use your hands. In another basin, beat the eggs till light and fluffy. Combine this with the fruit mixture and stir them well together. (Get everyone in the family to stir for good luck!) Cover the mixture and leave to stand overnight.

The next day, pour the pudding mixture into the basins and cover them with wax paper. Tie on pudding cloths or snap on your lids if you are using that type of basin. Steam for 6–8 hours, depending on the size. Re-heat on Christmas Day for a further 2 hours.

2 oz / 60 g / ¼ cup figs
6 oz / 180 g / ¼ cup currants
8 oz / 250 g / 1 cup seeded raisins
8 oz / 250 g / 1 cup sultanas
3 oz / 90 g / ⅜ cup dried apricots
3 oz / 90 g / ⅜ cup pitted dates
4 dessertspoonsful grated orange peel
2 dessertspoonsful grated lemon peel
4 oz / 125 g / 1 cup chopped almonds
3 fl oz / 150 ml / ⅔ cup orange juice
2 fl oz / 75 ml / ⅓ cup lemon juice
4 fl oz / 150 ml / ⅔ cup brandy
8 oz / 250 g / 2 cups plain wholemeal flour
1 lb / 500 g / 8 cups soft wholemeal bread-crumbs
1 lb / 500 g / 2⅔ cups Muscovado sugar
2 carrots, peeled and finely grated
2 apples, cored and finely chopped
1 tsp ground allspice
1 tsp ground cinnamon
1 tsp ground nutmeg
1 tsp salt
8 oz / 250 g / 1 cup vegetable suet or butter
6 eggs

Alternative Light Christmas Cake

6 oz / 180 g / ¾ cup butter or margarine
6 oz / 180 g / 1 cup light Muscovado sugar
3 large eggs
8 oz / 250 g / 2 cups plain wholemeal flour
4 oz / 125 g / ½ cup chopped dried
   pineapple
4 oz / 125 g / ½ cup chopped cherries
8 oz / 250 g / 1 cup sultanas
2 oz / 60 g / ¼ cup chopped dried apricots
   which have been soaked in 2 tbsps fresh
   orange juice
2 tbsp sherry
3 oz / 90 g / ¾ cup each chopped almonds
   and Brazil nuts

Cream the butter and sugar together until light and fluffy. Beat the eggs in a separate basin. Add the flour and egg alternately to the butter mixture. Add all the other ingredients and mix well. Pour into a greased and lined 8 inch (20 cm) cake tin, and bake in a 325°F / 170°C / Mark 3 oven for 1 hour. Then lower the temperature to 300°F / 160°C / Mark 2 for a further hour.

Mature Mincemeat (Vegetarian Variety)

8 oz / 250 g / vegetable suet
1 large cooking apple, grated
8 oz / 250 g / 1 cup currants
6 oz / 180 g / ¾ cup seeded raisins
2 oz / 60 g / ¼ cup chopped dates
1 oz / 30 g / ⅛ cup candied peel
juice and grated rind of 1 lemon
5 oz / 140 g / ⅞ cup Muscovado sugar
1 tsp ground allspice
1 oz / 30 g / ¼ cup ground almonds
½ tsp ground cinnamon
½ tsp ground cloves
¼ pint / 150 ml / ⅔ cup sherry
2 tbsp rum or brandy

Mix all the ingredients in a bowl together. Pack into clean jars, seal and store. If you are leaving it longer than a couple of weeks before using the mincemeat, bake the fruit mixture, excluding the alcohol, in a cool oven for about 3 hours to prevent fermentation. Cool the fruit, add the liquor and bottle.

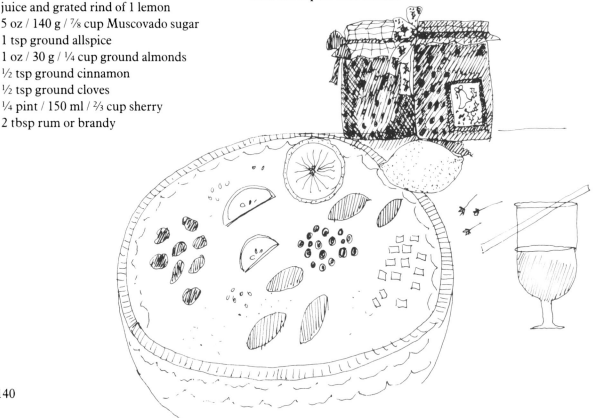

Parkin

This is a cake traditionally served on Guy Fawkes' Night to combat the cold. Make it a week before Bonfire Night to give it time to mature and get nice and sticky.

Sift the flour, salt, spices and bicarbonate of soda (or baking powder) into a bowl. Stir in the oats. Heat the molasses, butter, milk and sugar in a saucepan until dissolved. Allow to cool. Add the egg, and beat everything together. Make a well in the centre of the flour, pour in the molasses mixture and beat with a wooden spoon. When smooth, pour into a greased and lined 7 inch (18 cm) square baking tray. Bake for 50–60 minutes at 350°F / 180°C / Mark 4 until set and springy to the touch. Allow the parkin to cool in the tin for 10 minutes. Store in an airtight tin when cool.

6 oz / 180 g / 1½ cups plain wholewheat flour
1 tsp salt
3 tsp ground ginger
1 tsp ground cinnamon
1 tsp bicarbonate of soda
10 oz / 325 g / 4 cups rolled oats
6 fl oz / 180 ml / 1⅕ cup molasses
5 oz / 140 g / ⅞ cup butter
¼ pint / 150 ml / ⅔ cup milk
4 oz / 125 g / ⅔ cup Muscovado sugar
1 egg

DECEMBER

This is the month of goodwill to all men, which includes supplying endless tasty tit-bits for friends and relations who drop by to share your Christmas Spirit. So, included this month are some recipes for delicious nibbles to serve with the Blackcurrant Liqueur (page 93) and Blackberry Gin (page 128) that has been quietly maturing for the last few months. If you never got round to making it, don't worry – you can produce a large jug of Mulled Wine in under twenty minutes (page 153).

With the emphasis on entertaining, I have included a variety of recipes that I hope will prove once and for all that vegetarianism does not preclude sumptuous gourmet food! There is a special Christmas roast, a Cheese and Walnut Pâté, and Lentil Burgers and Cranberry Sauce; for a really impressive presentation, try the Vegetable Plait. For dessert, indulge yourself with the Carob Cashew Nut Mousse or the Truffle Plait. As most of the basic Christmas cooking was done in November, it leaves you time to try a few new recipes for the celebrations. It always seems more rewarding cooking for a crowd.

The scene in the garden is one of mainly root crops and cabbages. Brussel sprouts are available but are better once they have had a spot of frost on them. In the shops, the Christmas fruits are in good supply: satsumas, clementines, fresh nuts, chestnuts, dates and figs.

Don't, however, make your Christmas preparations so elaborate and impressive that you end up an exhausted wreck. Remember that it's a holiday and you are supposed to enjoy it!

With this in mind, do something just for you. Fill a muslin bag with chamomile flowers, lavender, and yarrow. Then, when you have finished preparing all your Christmas fare, slip up to the bathroom and run a nice relaxing bath. Hang the scented bag under the hot tap. This mixture should both calm you down and revive you.

Lentil and Vegetable Soup

2 tbsp oil
2 medium onions, chopped
1 leek, cleaned and chopped
1 parsnip, peeled and chopped
2 stalks of celery, chopped
2 large carrots, chopped
2 tbsp flour
4 pints / 2½ litres / 10 cups vegetable stock
1 lb / 500 g / ⅔ cups lentils (red, soaked overnight if possible)
14 oz / 400 ml /2 cups canned tomatoes
¼ tsp thyme

A thick and hearty soup, this is almost a meal in itself. The vegetables here are only a suggestion; use whatever takes your fancy.

In a large pan, heat the oil and sauté the onion until brown. Add all the remaining vegetables except the tomatoes, and sauté for 5 minutes. Stir in the flour, and cook for 3 minutes. Gradually add in the stock, stirring all the time to prevent lumps. Pour in the drained lentils, the tomatoes and thyme. Simmer gently for about an hour. Serve with some good crusty bread.

Tofu and Sesame Pâté

4 firm tomatoes, finely chopped
10 oz / 300 g / 2 cups plain tofu
1 tbsp tahini spread
3 oz / 90 g / ¾ cup roasted sesame seeds
1 tbsp chopped parsley
¼ tbsp ground horseradish
juice of ½ lemon
salt and pepper to taste

Mix all the ingredients together in a bowl. Spoon into separate pâté dishes, chill, and serve with melba toast or crackers.

Stilton Soup

1 medium onion, finely chopped
4 oz / 125 g / ½ cup butter
8 oz / 250 g / 2 cups Stilton or blue cheese
4 oz / 125 g / 1 cup plain flour
2 pints / 1¼ litres / 5 cups light vegetable stock
1 piece mace and 1 bay leaf
salt and pepper to taste
cream for serving

Beware! This will stick to the bottom of your saucepan, so watch the heat.

Fry the onion lightly in the butter until light brown. Stir in the cheese. When melted, add the flour and cook for a few minutes. Gradually add the stock, stirring continually. Add the mace, bay leaf, salt and pepper, and simmer very gently for 15 minutes. Remove the bay and mace. Pour into a serving dish, and top with the cream. Serve immediately.

Cheese and Walnut Pâté

Mix the cheese, beer, mustard, salt and pepper together in a bowl. Mix in the cayenne pepper and butter, and cream together. Stir in the walnuts. Press into a pâté dish. Cover the dish, then chill before serving.

8 oz / 250 g / 2 cups grated Cheddar cheese
⅛ pint / 75 ml / ⅓ cup beer
½ tsp ground mustard powder
salt and pepper to taste
¼ tsp cayenne pepper
4 oz / 125 g / ½ cup softened butter
2 oz / 60 g / ½ cup finely chopped walnuts

Asparagus Quiche

For the pastry, rub the margarine into the flour. Rub in the Parmesan cheese and cayenne pepper. Add 4 or 5 tbsp of cold water – enough to make a pliable dough. Roll out the pastry, and line a 10 inch (25 cm) flan dish. Prick the base and bake blind for 15 minutes at 425°F / 220°C / Mark 7.

Arrange the asparagus in the flan case. Beat the rest of the filling ingredients together, and pour over the top. Sprinkle with a little more cayenne pepper. Bake at reduced heat 375°F / 190°C / Mark 5 for 25–35 minutes until set.

Pastry
10 oz / 180 g / 2½ cups plain wholemeal flour
5 oz / 90 g / ⅝ cup vegetable margarine
1 oz / 30 g / ¼ cup grated Parmesan cheese
¼ tsp cayenne pepper

Filling
16 oz / 500 g / 2 cups canned asparagus spears
2 eggs
¼ pint / 150 ml / 1 cup milk
¼ pint / 150 ml / 1 cup single cream
salt and pepper to taste

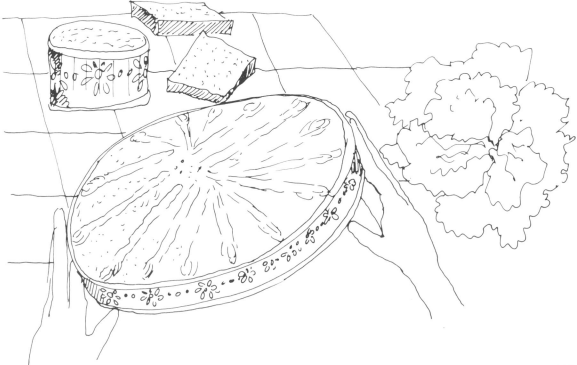

Chestnut and Peanut Christmas Roast

12 oz / 375 g / 2 cups dried chestnuts (soak
  overnight)
6 oz / 180 g / 1½ cups ground peanuts
8 oz / 250 g / 1½ cups cooked mashed potato
1 large onion, finely chopped
2 cloves garlic
4 oz / 125 g / 2 cups button mushrooms
2 eggs
1 tbsp shoyu
1 tsp basil
salt and pepper to taste

The vegetarian's answer to the turkey. You can cook this in any shaped vessel you choose to make it more interesting. A ring mould is a good idea as you can fill the centre with Fruity Stuffing (below) or with vegetables.

Boil the chestnuts for about an hour, then drain and purée them. Put them into a large mixing bowl. Stir in the peanuts and potato. Fry the onion and garlic in a little oil until soft. Add the mushrooms, and continue to cook gently until they are soft. Mix this into the other ingredients in the mixing bowl with the nuts, then add the rest of the ingredients. Grease a baking tin of your choice. It will take longer to cook in a small deep pan than in a roasting pan, so allow for this. Spoon the mixture into the pan and press down fairly firmly – this will help it turn out more easily and also make it easier to cut. Bake between 35–50 minutes until firm and brown at 350°F / 180°C / Mark 4.

Fruity Stuffing

6 oz / 180 g / ¾ cup dried prunes
6 oz / 180 g / ¾ cup dried apricots
1 medium onion, finely chopped
grated rind of 1 lemon
8 oz / 250 g / 4 cups wholemeal breadcrumbs
1 tsp dried tarragon
salt and pepper to taste
¼ pint / 150 ml / ⅔ cup vegetable stock

Serve this stuffing with the Christmas Roast.

Soak the prunes and apricots overnight. Drain them and chop into little pieces. In a large bowl, combine all the ingredients together. Either shape the stuffing into balls, and bake for 15 minutes at 375°F / 190°C / Mark 5, or put the mixture into a well greased, ovenproof dish and bake for 20 minutes at the same temperature.

Vegetable Plait

Prepare the pastry by rubbing the fat into the flour. Gradually add 3 or 4 tbsp cold water until you have a smooth, pliable dough. Leave to stand while you prepare the vegetables. Wash all the root vegetables and dice them. In a large pan, heat a little oil and sauté the root vegetables and celery for 6 minutes. Add boiling water, and cook for about 5 minutes – they should still be firm. Drain the vegetables and place in a bowl. Melt the butter in a pan, and sauté the onions, leeks and mushrooms, until they start to brown. Lift from the pan, and mix with the other vegetables.

In the pan with the butter reserved from cooking the onions, add the flour and cook for 3 minutes, stirring. Stir in the tomato purée, herbs and shoyu, then gradually add the milk, stirring all the time to prevent lumps. Add the cheese, and then stir this sauce into the vegetables.

Roll the pastry into an oblong shape then, on the long sides, make diagonal slits one third the width of the pastry. This will leave a column up the centre one third of the total width in which to put the filling. It is easier to finish off the plait if the pastry is put on the baking sheet before cutting. Carefully spread the vegetable mixture down the centre, and then begin the folding. Start by tucking the end pieces in. Then alternately cross the side pieces over to form a plait. Brush with beaten egg and bake for 25–45 minutes at 375°F / 190°C / Mark 5. Serve hot or cold.

Pastry
12 oz / 375 g / 3 cups plain wholemeal flour
6 oz / 190 g / ¾ cup vegetable margarine
beaten egg to glaze

Filling
12 oz / 375 g / 2 cups potatoes
8 oz / 250 g / 1½ cups carrots
4 oz / 125 g / 1 cup swede
4 oz / 125 g / 1 cup parsnips
4 oz / 125 g / 1 cup celery, sliced
2 oz / 60 g / ¼ cup butter or margarine
2 onions, finely chopped
1 leek, washed and sliced
4 oz / 125 g / 2 cups mushrooms, sliced
2 oz / 60 g / ½ cup plain flour
1 tsp tomato purée
1 heaped tbsp chopped parsley
¼ tsp ground bay leaves
1 tsp shoyu
1 pint / 625 ml / 2½ cups milk
4 oz / 125 g / 1 cup Cheddar cheese, grated

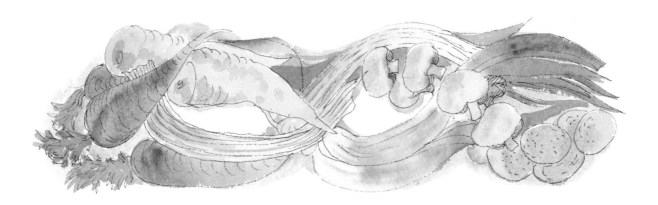

Festive Lentil Burgers and Cranberry Sauce

12 oz / 375 g / 2 cups continental lentils
¾ pint / 450 ml / 2 cups water
2 medium onions
6 oz / 190 g / 3 cups mushrooms, finely
   chopped
2 medium red peppers, chopped
1 clove garlic
2 tbsp chopped parsley
2 tbsp tomato purée
1 large egg
salt and pepper to taste
beaten egg and wholemeal breadcrumbs to
   coat

Cranberry Sauce
¼ pint / 150 ml / ⅔ cup water
4 oz / 125 g / ⅔ cup Demerara sugar
juice of 1 large orange
8 oz / 250 g / 2 cups fresh cranberries

Thoroughly wash the lentils. Put into a large saucepan with the water, and cook for about 30 minutes until soft. Fry the onion in a little oil until transparent. Add the mushrooms and peppers, and continue to cook until soft. Stir in the tomato purée with the vegetables. Mash the lentils until smooth. Add the other ingredients. Shape into burgers, brush with beaten egg, roll in wholemeal breadcrumbs, and fry in oil until golden brown.

For the sauce, put the water, sugar and orange juice into a saucepan, and heat through gently to dissolve the sugar. Stir in the cranberries, and bring back to the boil. Reduce the heat and simmer for 10 minutes. Serve with the burgers.

Fantail Roast Potatoes

2 or 3 medium potatoes per person
oil for roasting
salt and pepper to taste

This gives roast potatoes a rather fancier appearance.

Peel the potatoes and slice them ¾ the way through along their length in a fan effect. Place in an oiled baking tray, and brush the tops with oil. Season well, and bake for 1 hour at 350°F / 180°C / Mark 4 until cooked through.

Duchesse Potatoes

1½ lb / 750 g / 5 cups peeled potatoes
2 egg yolks
3 tbsp butter or margarine
salt and pepper to taste
beaten egg to glaze

These make a lovely accompaniment for the Christmas lunch – a change from or supplement to roast potatoes.

Cook the potatoes until tender. Mash, and then stir in the egg yolks and butter. Season. Using a piping tube with a large nozzle, pipe rosettes of potato onto a greased baking sheet. Brush with the egg, and bake in a 375°F / 190°C / Mark 5 oven for 10–15 minutes until golden brown.

Sprouts with Carrots

Trim the sprouts and mark a cross in the bottoms. Peel and slice the carrots lengthways. Put the vegetables into a saucepan of boiling salted water, and boil for only 10 minutes so that they still have bite to them. Melt the butter in another pan, and add the flaked almonds. Fry until golden brown. Pour the vegetables into a serving dish, and then toss in the almonds over the top.

1 lb / 500 g / 4 cups medium Brussel sprouts
1 lb / 500 g / 3 cups carrots
2 oz / 60 g / ¼ cup butter or margarine
1 oz / 30 g / ¼ cup flaked almonds
salt and pepper to taste

Red Cabbage Salad

Finely grate the red cabbage. De-seed the peppers and dice them. Shred the watercress, discarding the stalks. Put all the vegetables into a salad bowl with the oranges and raisins. Put all the ingredients for the dressing into a blender. Run the machine until the dressing is smooth. Pour over the salad and toss.

1 lb / 500 g / 4 cups red cabbage
2 medium red peppers
1 large bunch watercress
6 oz / 180 g / 3 cups button mushrooms
2 large oranges, peeled and segmented
2 oz / 60 g / ¼ cup raisins

Dressing
¼ pint / 150 ml / ⅔ cup sunflower oil
2 tbsp cider vinegar
1 bunch watercress
1 egg
salt and pepper to taste
½ tsp Muscovado sugar
⅛ tsp dried thyme
⅛ tsp dried dill weed

Bean Salad

Soak the beans overnight in separate bowls. Drain and rinse them in the morning. Cook the beans in separate pans to prevent the colours running. This will take between 1–1½ hours. Drain the beans, and allow to cool completely. Put the other ingredients in a large screw-top jar, and shake vigorously until well blended. Pour the dressing over the beans and toss all together.

3 oz / 90 g / ½ cup red kidney beans
3 oz / 90 g / ½ cup haricot beans
3 oz / 90 g / ½ cup flageolet beans
3 oz / 90 g / ½ cup black-eyed peas
1 medium onion, finely chopped
1 clove garlic, crushed
1 tbsp chopped parsley
½ tsp dried savory
salt and pepper to taste
4 fl oz / 125 ml / ½ cup sunflower oil
1 fl oz / 30 ml / 2 tbsps white wine vinegar

Apricot and Peanut Salad

4 oz / 125 g / ½ cup dried apricots, soaked
  overnight
3 dessert apples
12 oz / 375 g / 3 cups grated white cabbage
4 oz / 125 g / ½ cup salted roasted peanuts

Dressing
2 tsp. smooth peanut butter
¼ pint / 150 ml / ⅔ cup sunflower oil

Chop the apricots. Core and dice the apples, leaving the peel on. Put both into a salad bowl with the cabbage and peanuts. Put the ingredients for the dressing into a screw-top jar, and shake vigorously until thick and blended. Pour the dressing over the salad, toss and serve.

Crunchy Mustard

2 tbsp white mustard seed
2 tbsp black mustard seed
About ¼ pint / 150 ml / ⅔ cup white wine
  vinegar
3 level tbsp clear honey (use one that does
  not have too strong a flavour)
1 tsp salt
¼ tsp ground cinnamon

Make this to serve with your savoury dishes, or make it to give as an original present.

Soak the mustard seed in the vinegar overnight, or for at least for 12 hours. Reserve a tablespoonful of the seeds and then put the remainder with the vinegar into a blender with the honey, salt and cinnamon. Blend until thick and creamy. If the mustard seems too thick add a little more vinegar. Stir in the remaining mustard seeds. Pot the mustard into clean pots and cover very tightly, otherwise it will shrink.

Spiced Chick Peas

8 oz / 250 g / 1⅓ cups chick peas, soaked
  overnight
sea salt
¼ tsp cumin
⅛ tsp coriander
⅛ tsp fenugreek

This Christmas, be a bit more adventurous with your party tit-bits. These Spiced Chick Peas and the Tamari Nuts and Raisins on the following page are a tasty alternative to the same old crisps and salted peanuts – less expensive, too!

Drain the peas and put them into a pan of fresh water. Simmer them for about 2 hours until just tender. Drain well. Oil a baking sheet. Sprinkle the peas with sea salt and the spices and then roast for 20 minutes at 350°F / 175°C / Mark 4. You can use tamari instead of spices if you prefer.

Tamari Nuts and Raisins

Spread a mixture of nuts on a large baking sheet. Almonds, cashews and sunflower seeds are a good choice. Bake for about 30 minutes at 350°F / 180°C / Mark 4 until golden brown. Remove the tray from the oven and stir in some raisins. Sprinkle with tamari while still hot – they should be quite salty.

Carob and Cashew Nut Mousse

3 oz / 90 g / bar carob 'chocolate'
4 oz / 125 g / ½ cup light Muscovado sugar
5 eggs, separated
4 oz / 125 g / 1 cup ground roasted cashew nuts
½ pint / 300 ml / 2 cups double cream
3 tbsp white wine vinegar
1 tsp Muscovado sugar
salt and pepper to taste

Break the carob bar into pieces into a basin. Add 4 tbsp water, and stand the basin in a saucepan of boiling water. Add the sugar, and stir this altogether until the carob has melted. Remove from the heat, and beat in the egg yolks one at a time. Stir the nuts into the carob mixture. Beat the cream until thick, and stir the carob mixture into it. Beat the egg whites until they form peaks. Carefully fold them into the carob mixture. Pour the mousse into a large bowl or 6 individual ones. Chill and serve. Decorate with extra cream if you wish.

Truffle Plait

Rich Shortcrust Pastry
8 oz / 250 g / 2 cups plain wholemeal flour
4 oz / 125 g / ½ cup margarine
1 oz / 30 g / ⅙ cup Muscovado sugar
1 egg yolk

Filling
8 oz / 250 g / 4 cups wholewheat sponge cake, crumbled
1 heaped tsp carob powder
1 tbsp boiling water
4 rounded tbsp mincemeat

Make the pastry by rubbing the fat into the flour until it looks like breadcrumbs. Gently rub in the sugar. Stir in the egg yolk with a knife. Add enough cold water to make a good pliable dough – about 4 tablespoons. Leave to rest for a while.

Make the filling by crumbling the cake into a bowl. Mix the carob powder in the boiling water in another bowl. Add this to the cake crumbs with the mincemeat and stir. Roll the pastry into an oblong then, on the long sides, make diagonal slits one third the width of the pastry. This will leave a column up the centre one third of the total width; spoon the filling onto this. 'Plait' the pastry, crossing the side pieces over. Brush milk for a glaze along the top. Bake at 425°F / 220°C / Mark 7 for 25–30 minutes.

Chestnut Cream

This is an alternative pudding topping to brandy butter.

Whisk the cream and stir in the chestnut purée, sugar and orange liqueur.

8 fl oz / 300 ml / 2 cups whipping cream
1 x 14 oz / 400 g / 2 cups canned
    unsweetened chestnut purée
2 tbsp light Muscovado sugar (run through
    a blender to make it finer)
3 tbsp Grand Marnier liqueur

Cranberry Mousse

If you use tofu in this recipe it will be suitable for vegans.

Gently stew the cranberries until tender. You may need to add some water. Liquidize in small amounts with the tofu or yogurt and honey. Fill six dishes and decorate the tops with a few cranberries.

1 lb / 500 g / 3 cups cranberries (reserve a
    few for decoration)
10 oz / 300 g / 2 cups soft tofu or 10 oz / 300 g
    / 2 cups thick yogurt
honey to taste

Mulled Wine

A little something to keep the masses quiet when they first arrive or to serve as a warming drink on your return from Carol Singing. To make it even easier to make mulled wine, it is possible to buy little spiced Gluhwein Bags.

Put the sugar in a large saucepan with ¼ pint / 150 ml / ⅔ cup water and slowly dissolve. Add the cinnamon, cloves, orange rind, orange slices and wine and bring very slowly to the boil. Remove from the heat immediately and leave to infuse for 10 minutes. Strain into a jug and serve.

1 bottle cheap red wine
2 tbsp Demerara sugar
1 cinnamon stick
6 cloves
2 thin strips of pithless orange rind
1 orange, sliced

GROWING BEANSPROUTS

Beansprouts are an excellent source of vitamins and minerals, and add variety to everyday meals in the winter. They are useful for sandwich fillings and a good base for a salad, as well as being delicious on their own.

You do not need special equipment. The basic requirements are large glass jars, some muslin or similar cloth to fix over the neck of the jar; and something to tie the cloth on with. You have to be able to rinse the beans without losing half of them down the sink.

If you only want to sprout beans on a small scale, you can purchase a special seed sprouting tray. It is layered so that you can sprout several varieties at once. It is possible to sprout many different types of beans, seeds, lentils and peas. They must be whole, as the split ones do not sprout. Start with mung beans, as they are the most familiar. They are the ones used in Chinese cooking although it is difficult to sprout them to the same length – you need to force them for that.

Always rinse your beans before sprouting. It is better still if you can soak them overnight, as this will speed the sprouting time. Use cold boiled water to soak; the chlorine in tap water can inhibit the growth of the beans.

Rinse the beans thoroughly after soaking. Drain them well and put into a jar. Keep the beans in as dark a place as possible, as this speeds sprouting. Remember to rinse them thoroughly twice a day. Keep them in a warm environment – at least 158°F / 70°C. They should be ready after between 3 and 5 days, according to the variety. Here is a list of a few of the most popular beans, how much to use and their time taken to sprout:

ALFALFA: use 3 or 4 tablespoons seed, and eat when 1½ inches (4 cm) long, after about 5 days.

MUNG: 1 handful. Eat when ½ inch (1.25 cm) up to 2½ inch (6 cm). Takes about 5 days.

SUNFLOWER SEEDS: 1 handful. Eat when the sprout is the same length as the seed.

FENUGREEK: is lovely and spicy tasting. Sprout 1 handful and eat at about 1 inch (2.5 cm) long.

GREEN OR BROWN LENTILS: use a handful. Eat at 1½ inches (4 cm).

ADUKI BEANS: use a handful, and sprout until 1–1½ inches (2.5–4 cm) – about 5 days.

SESAME SEEDS: use a handful. They need only two days sprouting, and give very fine sprouts.

VEGETABLE SEEDS

Here is a short list of vegetable seeds which are good to grow. Seeds, like anything else, tend to go out of fashion, and each year there are new seeds available. The range of available seed is much more vast in America.

Artichokes (Jerusalem)
This is a species of perennial sunflower. These nobbly little vegetables are handy for putting into stews. They also make a good screen while they are growing. *American Variety:* Artichoke Green Globe Improved.

Beetroot
Simple to grow and delicious hot or cold. Boltardy, which as the name implies, is slow to go to seed. Cooks Delight is a beetroot that does not bleed. Sutton's Early Bunch which you plant in April is ready to eat in June.
American Varieties: Red Ace Hybrid which is an easy grower, Little Ball, a baby beet, and Detroit Red, an excellent all rounder.

Broad Beans / Fava Beans
The Sutton is a prolific cropper; Red Epicure is another good brand.
American Variety: Witkiem Major

Runner Beans / Pole Beans
Streamline is an old favourite. Sutton's Sunset is a fast growing variety; The Tzar is another trusty old timer. *American Varieties:* Romano has a distinctive taste and is excellent for freezing. Selma Zebrina is an early maturer and heavy yielder.

French Beans / Bush Beans
Masterpiece, Purley King and The Prince.
American Varieties: Tendercrop, Venture Blue Lake and Topcrop.

Broccoli
Purple Sprouting and Autumn Spear will crop for most of the year.
American Varieties: Broccoli Emperor and Early Emerald Hybrid.

Brussel Sprouts
Peer Gynt, New Year and Bedford Winter Harvest.
American Varieties: Green Marvel Hybrid, Prince Marvel Hybrid and an unusual Red Sprout, named Rubine.

Cabbage
Greyhound, Summer Monarch, Velocity, Winningstadt and Christmas Drumhead.
American Varieties: Darkin Hybrid, Tropic Giant Hybrid and Savoy King Hybrid.

Calabrese
This is a type of Broccoli. Express Corona and Autumn Spear.

Carrots
Early Nantes, Nantes Scarlet Horn, Autumn King, Early Giant, New Red and Sutton's Intermediate.
American Varieties: Aplus Hybrid is a carrot with a higher than average vitamin A content. Amstel is a small gourmet carrot; Nantes Coreless is another good seed.

Cauliflower
Sutton's Snow White, All the Year Round and Pinnacle.
American Varieties: Snow King, Alert and Romanasco, which has a conical shape.

Celeriac
This is a variety of celery, with a root like a turnip. Good seeds are Giant Prague and Tellus, which is a quick grower.

Celery
Ivory Tower and Solid White.
American Variety: Utah 52–70 Improved.

Chicory
Sugar Loaf, similar to Cos lettuce in looks with a good firm heart.
American Variety: Radicchio Giulio.

Courgettes / Zucchini
Zucchini and Green Bush Smallpak.

Cucumbers
Telegraph for the greenhouse or frame and Burpless Tasty Green for outdoor growing.
American Varieties: Sweet Success Hybrid, Euro-American Hybrid, Burpless Tasty Green, are available in the United States also.

Garlic
You can buy cloves from your seed merchant, but I

buy mine at the greengrocers. Separate the cloves and plant them.

Kale

Try Thousand Head and the very hardy Tall Green Curled.
American Varieties: Winterbor Hybrid and Dwarf Blue Curled Scotch varieties.

Kohl Rabi

This has a flavour which is a cross between cabbage and turnip. Examples are White Vienna which has solid white flesh and Purple Vienna which has a purple bulb.
American Varieties: Grand Duke and Rapid.

Leeks

Musselburgh, Lyon, Winter Crop.
American Variety: American Flag.

Lettuce

Sow these in small batches so they do not all mature together. Webb's Wonderful is a slow bolter. All Year Round is very hearty; Tom Thumb is an early maturer, with tight small heads. Little Gem is for those who like Cos/Romaine lettuce.
American Varieties: Buttercrunch, a variety with thick juicy leaves. Mission, which is an Iceberg type. Or add a bit of colour to the salad plate with an interesting red lettuce, Selma Lallo.

Marrow / Squash

White Bush and Long Green Trailing.
American Varieties: Jersey Golden Acorn is a good dual-purpose plant, delicious raw when young, and cooked when older. Butterblossom bears many male flowers, which are ideal for stuffing. Kuta Hybrid is a squash with a lovely buttery taste.

Onions

Onion sets (baby onions) are the easiest way to grow these. Rocardo is a good variety, as are Ailsa Craig and Rijnsburger. Spring onion varieties include White Lisbon and Winter Hardy, which you can sow in Autumn for Spring. Aviv and Paris Silverskin are small onions suitable for pickling.
American Varieties: Sweet Winter; this can be sown in areas of very low temperature to grow through the winter. Carmen Hybrid is a very good-flavoured red onion. For Scallions, try Evergreen White Bunching.

Crystal Wax Pickling is grown, as the name implies, for pickling.

Parsnips

Tender and True, White Gem.

Peas

Early varieties include Early Onward, Feltham First and Sweetness. Second Early: Sutton's Achievement, Eaton and Onward. Maincrop: Senator and Lord Chancellor. For delicious mangetout peas, sow Oregon Sugar Pod. Waverex is an excellent variety for freezing.
American Varieties: Maestro and Little Marvel. Second Early: Try Novella, a new type which is self-supporting when grown in a double row. "Petit Pois" Giray is a variety to grow for baby peas. Sugar Snap is a pea which can be eaten at all stages, pod as well, or Green Array, a prolific producer. For Snow Peas, try Blizzard.

Potatoes

Potatoes are a very effective way of clearing rough ground. Plant varieties of potato which are ready at different times. Maincrop, for the bulk of your crop, are the potatoes that you lift in October and should see you through until the next year. Record has a good flavour and is suitable for all types of cooking. King Edwards are great for jacket potatoes but are susceptible to disease. Desiree, the potato with the red skin, is extremely popular and appears to be quite slug-resistant.
Second Early: You can start to dig these as soon as the flowers start opening. Maris Peer and Arran Consul are both good.
American varieties: potatoes with an excellent keeping quality include Krantz, which are good for baking, boiling and chips, and La Rouge, which is a Red skin variety.
First Earlies: Home Guard and Epicure are two reliable varieties. These potatoes are ideal for digging to scrape or boil in their skins.

Sweet Potato varieties include Vardaman, which has wonderful cropping abilities and is perfect for the small garden. New Jewel is a slightly smaller variety which stores well.

Radish

Scarlet Globe, Cherry Belle, and Saxa.

American Varieties: Inca, Snow Belle Hybrid or French Breakfast.

Salsify
A little grown vegetable with a delicate flavour. Giant is the most commonly grown variety.

Spinach
Perpetual Spinach, Long Standing Round and New Zealand.
American Varieties: Basella, Malabar, Red Stem, Summer Special.

Swede/Rutabaga
Marian and Sutton's Western Perfection.

Sweetcorn
First of All, Kelvedon Glory and Candle.
American Varieties: Butterfruit, Seneca, Chief and Merit.

Swiss Chard
Lucullus Light Green and Swiss Chard of Geneva.

Tomatoes
Under glass try Alicante, Shirley and Big Boy. Outdoors try Moneymaker, or Tornado, which is specially bred for English weather conditions. Tiny Tim is a variety which you could grow in a window box.
American Varieties: Early season: Early Girl. Main crop: Park's Whopper, Mountain Pride, Burpee, Big Boy, Celebrity. Cherry: Sugar Lump.

Turnip
Snowball, Golden Ball, and Green Globe, which is the best variety to grow if you wish to eat the tops.
American Varieties: White Lady Hybrid, or Purple Top White Globe which has sweet white flesh.

INDEX